TO THE RESCUE

TO THE

Found Dogs with a Mission

RESCUE

Elise Lufkin

Photographs by **Diana Walker**

Foreword by
Bonnie Hunt

Skyhorse Publishing

Skyhorse Publishing books may be purchased in bulk at special discounts for sales promotion, corporate gifts, fund-raising, or educational purposes. Special editions can also be created to specifications. For details, contact the Special Sales Department, Skyhorse Publishing, 555 Eighth Avenue, Suite 903, New York, NY 10018 or info@skyhorsepublishing.com.

www.skyhorsepublishing.com

10 9 8 7 6 5 4 3 2 1

AUTHOR'S NOTE:
All profits from *To the Rescue* will be donated to groups researching and supporting the human-animal bond and to animal welfare organizations.

Library of Congress Cataloging-in-Publication Data
Lufkin, Elise.
To the rescue : found dogs with a mission/Elise Lufkin ;
photographs by Diana Walker ; foreword by Bonnie Hunt.
   p. cm.

Includes index.
ISBN 978-1-60239-772-9 (alk. paper)

1. Service dogs—Anecdotes. 2. Human-animal relationships—Anecdotes. I. Title.

HV1569.6.L84 2009
362.4'0483—dc22

2009012164

Printed in China

Contents

Acknowledgments

I am grateful to my editor, Lilly Golden, for suggesting the subject matter for *To the Rescue* and for all her help in making the book a reality. I am indebted to Tony Lyons of Skyhorse Publishing for supporting this book in the most valuable way of all—by publishing it. Colleen Daly worked with me throughout the project giving invaluable advice and encouragement. Laurie Leman has shown patience, perseverance, and skill in keeping everything straight. Others have contributed in important ways—my thanks to Jamie Lee Curtis, Bonnie Hunt, Jill Bentler, Fran Jewell, Kevin Kendrick, and Sue Lavoie. I am grateful to my friend, the talented Diana Walker, for her beautiful and moving photographs. Diana and I would like to thank Michele Stephenson, who with her discerning eye edited the pictures for this book.

Many generous people sent me interesting and inspiring stories about their dogs—my gratitude to them for the stories included in *To the Rescue* as well as for those on the Web site, www.founddogs.com.

Foreword

When I considered writing the foreword for this book, it took me about one second to say "yes." My immediate enthusiasm was due to not only the subject of the book, but also the intent of the author. Elise Lufkin has made a choice to make a difference.

My own life has been so positively and emotionally enhanced by the stray and shelter dogs I have adopted. The moment you make the commitment to rescue a dog and take on the rewarding responsibility of nurturing this new family member, you beam like a new parent and cherish the precious pup's soul.

The heartwarming stories and photos of these service dogs in *To the Rescue* will strike an emotional chord that I hope will encourage many to adopt a stray, donate to a shelter, or simply share the stories within these pages. You will appreciate Elise shedding light on the fact that there are shelters full of dogs with great potential, just waiting to be given a chance. As you will read within these pages, these dogs welcome the opportunity to be of service. These service dogs bring a deep emotional connection and specific life services, that are heroic at times—guiding the blind, therapeutic visits to children's hospitals, and search and rescue. The services they provide can change a life from dependent to independent, from lonely to fulfilled, and in some cases even make the difference between life and death.

If you have ever been blessed with the unconditional love of a pet, this book will bring you great joy and comfort. If you have not shared the love, joy, and warmth of having a dog—any dog, but especially a rescue or stray dog—in your life, this book will give you the insight and, hopefully, the nudge to give a needy dog a chance.

You will be inspired by the celebrated intelligence of these once abandoned dogs, and the instant love, help, and specific abilities they bring to those in need of assistance.

The ideal of dedication and loyalty is defined in this book. It comes to life in these stories. Enjoy, and remember to share the heartwarming truth that stray dogs, shelter dogs, all dogs deserve a chance to love and be loved.

Bonnie Hunt
actress/writer/producer/director/
and host of *The Bonnie Hunt Show*

Introduction

Throughout my life, I have been involved with animals—dogs, cats, horses, even snakes. I can't remember a time in my life without a dog. The Christmas card my parents sent the year I was born is a photograph of a plump, smiling baby trying to pull herself up on a large and very patient dog. When I was ten, a small terrier mix turned up at our house and captivated six children in about five minutes. She then set out to charm my parents, a more difficult challenge that took the better part of a day. Sweetie Pie stayed with us for fifteen years. Dogs shared the exuberance and fun of my childhood and comforted me through bouts of painful shyness. Fortunately, there was always a dog to turn to for solace.

Diana Walker, photographer and creator of the touching images in this book, has also shared her life with dogs and understands their capacity to enhance our existence. Diana's life has always included dogs; one of her earliest memories is of the family Norwich terrier, Strawberry, giving birth to a litter of puppies in the basement. Diana is quick to point out that her love for dogs has in no way smothered, or even affected, her passion for cats—fifty years of cats: Abdul, Daisy, Fred, and Ginger.

Dogs have enriched my life immeasurably. Working with them has taught me a great deal. Some years ago I initiated a program at my local animal shelter where volunteers worked with dogs to socialize them. The dogs received some basic obedience training to make them more attractive as candidates for adoption and more successful in their new homes. Through this work, I saw in a concrete way the tragedy of pet overpopulation, and I began to realize how many

dogs with real potential are languishing in animal shelters all around the country. I was horrified to learn how many dogs must be killed every year to make room for the next batch of unwanted animals.

Partly in reaction to this bleak side of the work, I began to focus on the happy endings, the success stories. I have always been interested in the bond between people and dogs. Shelter work showed me the special relationship that often blossoms when an animal is rescued. Truly, one man's trash can be another man's treasure.

My two previous books, *Found Dogs: Tales of Strays Who Landed on Their Feet* and *Second Chance: More Tales of Found Dogs,* are collections of stories about rescued dogs and the many ways in which those dogs reward the kind and generous people who have helped them. In the foreword for *Found Dogs,* Peter Mayle writes, "But when you adopt a dog . . . very little is certain—except, of course, that you will be giving him a better life. And he will be doing the same for you." *To the Rescue* continues and extends the subject. It is a collection of stories about unwanted animals—pound dogs, shelter dogs, and random strays—that find good homes with people who help them to become therapy dogs and service dogs. (I have included one brave cat as well.)

Therapy animals visit hospitals, nursing homes, prisons, mental health facilities, hospice programs, and other places where days can seem long and dreary, and distraction is welcome. For many years I took my dog, Posy, for weekly visits at our local nursing home. Posy had many fans there, and she loved spending time with them.

She would begin to dance around in the back-seat of the car whenever we approached the turn leading into the home's parking lot. She knew that she was important to her friends, and she always enjoyed an appreciative audience. Anyone who loves dogs knows that they can make happy times happier and difficult times more bearable. Dogs give us so much pleasure; they comfort us and make us laugh. Just petting them can lower our blood pressure. Soothing physical contact is therapeutic for all of us: Think of stroking a dog's soft ears or holding a purring cat.

Dogs also work with professional therapists toward specific goals. In physical and occupational therapy programs, patients practice motor skills while brushing and petting a dog, and work on balance while walking with a dog. An enthusiastic dog can motivate a patient to throw a ball or use hand signals to indicate which trick in the dog's repertoire will bring a biscuit reward. Dogs can serve as an icebreaker, encouraging conversation between patient and therapist and among people in a group setting. A friendly dog can increase a person's self-esteem. Dogs can help teach children and teenagers about nurturing behavior and empathy; they can be especially effective with at-risk children and teenagers.

Then there are service dogs. According to the Americans with Disabilities Act, a dog is considered a service dog if it has been "individually trained to do work or perform tasks for the benefit of a person with a disability." Guide dogs for the blind, hearing dogs, dogs that alert their owners to an impending seizure or heart attack, dogs that help people walk, that open doors, turn on lights, fetch the phone, and pick up dropped objects—all are service dogs. For *To the Rescue*, I have stretched the term "service dog" to include dogs that perform many kinds of activities that help people, for example, search-and-rescue dogs, avalanche dogs, dogs that detect narcotics or bombs, even some dogs that are trained to find bedbugs!

White working on *Found Dogs* and *Second Chances* I was impressed and moved by the compassion, generosity, and love many people give to abandoned animals, animals that have sometimes been discarded like old Kleenex. In the case of *To the Rescue*, these people give more than a good home. First they provide a new life for a dog that needs one, then they help that dog to be productive, often bringing comfort and happiness to people. Rescue alone involves a lot of work: care and feeding, medical attention, and obedience training to help the animal learn to live comfortably with people. After all that effort, most of us would relax and simply enjoy life with our nice, well-behaved dog.

Some people however, go further: They train their dogs to help others. Dogs for therapy work are usually screened first to be sure that they will be calm and comfortable in different situations. They often must pass a Canine Good Citizen test or the equivalent. This test requires that the dog display competence in basic obedience; they must be able to sit, stay, come, and walk on a leash without pulling, all this while ignoring distractions. The dog must be quiet and well-behaved, and must be calm around other dogs. The handler learns to interact with all types of patients in a variety of settings, such as hospitals, nursing homes, and schools. More training may be required for dogs that work with therapists, such as physical therapists, occupational therapists, and mental health professionals. Dogs in search-and-rescue or detection of narcotics or bombs (or bedbugs) require a great deal of training in their area of expertise.

Once the dog's training is accomplished and certification achieved, the handler then agrees to take that dog on a regular basis to help others, whether in hospital visits or search-and-rescue work. Whatever the dog does, ongoing training is part of the package. This is a big commitment of time and energy. Billie Peters, who tells her story in *To the Rescue*, takes her rescued racing greyhounds to visit a nursing home, a veterans' hospital, and a children's reading program. Billie is in her eighties.

In a world where we see cruelty and neglect everywhere, it is heartening to hear stories of people who are compassionate, generous, and kind. It is inspiring to see the remarkable healing effect animals can have on people, and the many benefits of the bond between the two.

BAILEY

—— *Eileen Roemer, FBI special agent, retired* ——

When we got Bailey, he was infested with fleas and ticks and was emaciated, literally starving to death. He was supposedly being used as a golden retriever stud dog by an unscrupulous breeder. Three times he managed to dig a hole under the fence and escape; after Bailey's third successful breakout, the animal control officer agreed to let me rescue him. Immediately, I took him to the vet, and his new life began.

At the time I was working for the FBI in behavior analysis, specializing in child abduc-

tion. One of my primary duties was acting as liaison with victims' families. I adopted Bailey for one of these families, but he had some adjustment problems. When they decided that they couldn't keep him, they gave him to me. He settled in quickly, perhaps because of the other two dogs I had.

When my first search dog, Riley, also a golden, was a puppy, I took a course in body recovery at the FBI. Shortly afterward I met a woman with dogs in Search and Rescue (SAR), and I was fascinated. I decided to train and certify Riley in SAR as a cadaver dog. From my work with victims' families, I knew how essential body recovery was for bringing closure to family and friends. Riley passed all the certification tests. She loved the work, and she was good at it. My husband and I have another rescued golden, Annie. I trained her, but she has multiple anxieties and never really enjoyed the work.

When Bailey came along, I realized he had the intense play drive necessary for the challenges of SAR. He took to the process naturally: To him it's a fascinating and compelling game and an opportunity to play. I always keep one of those pink-and-green soft Frisbees as a special reward for search work. We trained every Sunday, and each time we went out I learned something new about a dog's abilities and how to read their body language, for example, noting very slight head movements as the wind shifted.

In due course Bailey became certified for SAR. His first real job was searching at the Pentagon after 9/11. I'm a Navy Reservist, and that day I was on duty at the Pentagon.

I left the building at 7:30 AM. The person who replaced me was killed along with thirty-four others. For twelve days I worked with Bailey and Riley, alternating them in searches for human remains. It was tough because we were looking for people I knew. We worked with piles of rubble brought from the Pentagon to a parking lot. We would make one pass, then the evidence people would go in with rakes. There was an overwhelming smell of jet fuel, mixed with an overwhelming smell of death, but both dogs knew just what to do, identifying minute fragments of human remains. There was so much stuff there, so many scents. I was amazed at how focused the dogs were.

Of course the dogs' noses were down there in all that toxic debris. At least we handlers had masks. Periodically we were decontaminated, while vets and vet techs decontaminated the dogs in wading pools. After that I would bring out the Frisbee for some playtime and relaxation, as rewards for good work. Then we would search through the same rubble a second time. Bailey made many, many finds, and even though this is not her story, I have to say that Riley did too.

Bailey is retired now. He must be twelve or thirteen, but he can still jump up on the bed. When he sees that Frisbee, or if I bring out his search jacket, he dances around, bursting with excitement and happiness. He's a sweet boy, Mr. B.

I feel very lucky that I chanced upon this work with the dogs. It is one of the most important things I have done in my life, and Bailey has been a big part of it.

MAGGIE

—— Al Emond, Retired elementary school principal ——

The day that I retired after thirty-two years as a teacher, counselor, and elementary school principal, I went to the dog pound. There was Maggie, a shepherd-collie mix, about two years old, lying on the cement floor with her head on her paws, looking at me. I bent down to talk to her, and her tail wagged a little. When she stood up, I noticed a big gash on her hip. The attendant put a leash on the dog, and we walked a little until she stopped and leaned against me. Then she lay down with her head and one paw across my feet. I thought, *Uh-oh, she's choosing me!*

I was afraid no one would adopt her with that injury, and, anyway, it was love at first sight. Apparently, Maggie had been struck by a car two weeks before, and when animal control went to pick her up she was lying unconscious in the street with a large open gash on her right rear leg. She had just been put up for adoption; if no one took her during the next seven days, she would be put to sleep. I agreed to pick her up the next day. At home I made an appointment with the veterinarian for the following Monday.

The next day, a Saturday, I brought Maggie home. As she checked out the house and the backyard, I noticed that she was walking slowly and breathing heavily. I figured that she was exhausted and just needed a meal and a good rest in a warm, comfortable bed; however by Sunday afternoon I could see that her health was deteriorating. She was restless during the night, and had trouble lying down and getting up. First thing Monday morning I called the veterinarian. The doctor couldn't believe that the shelter had not had their veterinarian suture the gash on Maggie's leg; after two weeks it was now too late for sutures. He took X-rays and ran some tests. The X-rays showed that Maggie had a torn diaphragm muscle from her accident with the car. Her lower organs were pushing up against her heart and lungs. On top of all this, she was about three weeks from having a litter of puppies. The veterinarian told me that I had a choice to make: I could have the dog put down then and there, or attempt major, expensive surgery with a specialist. There was no guarantee she would pull through.

Maggie had been with me less than two days, but I had grown to love her. She was already under my skin—she was my responsibility. She seemed to have had a purpose

even though I wasn't sure what that purpose might be.

I took Maggie to the specialist right away, who explained to me that besides the torn diaphragm muscle, one of the puppies had broken through the uterus wall, pressing against Maggie's heart. The surgery would have to be immediate and would cost $3,000. I said, "Let's do it!" I told her she was going to be O.K., and left the hospital with tears running down my face.

Five hours later the doctor called to say that the surgery had been successful but that all the puppies were dead. Two days later Maggie came home wearing an Elizabethan collar. During her recuperation, Maggie and I bonded even more. I kept saying to myself, "I know this dog has a purpose."

A few weeks later I read about a Delta Society Pet Partners course to train animals and owners to be pet therapy teams. This was Maggie's purpose! For years I thought of owning a therapy dog to visit hospitals, convalescent homes, and schools. Maggie was a friendly, happy dog that loved people. She liked to give kisses, to lean against you, and to get as close as she possibly could. She was perfect for the job. I took the course, and Maggie and I worked on all the basics—sit, down, stay, and some leash work. Maggie passed the certification test with flying colors. Our first job consisted of weekly visits to a first grade reading program. Individual students would read to Maggie, who always looked interested and nonjudgmental. As a reward, the children were allowed to give Maggie treats and take her for a walk.

Four months later Maggie needed another surgery, this time to resuture the diaphragm muscle. After she had recuperated, our pet therapy instructor asked us to visit a convalescent home: We have been volunteering there for over five years. We also make occasional visits to local hospitals.

During the past two years Maggie has developed two other medical problems. She has a rare form of diabetes, treatable with daily medication. She also developed dry eye syndrome in her right eye. The tear duct did not work properly; after numerous unsuccessful attempts with different medications over a period of five months, she underwent surgery to connect the salivary gland to the tear duct in order to provide moisture to lubricate the eye. This worked perfectly, although when she is particularly excited about treats or dinner, her right eye does weep a little.

Throughout all these trials, Maggie has lost none of her spirit. Her extended family, the residents of the convalescent home, has supported her all the way, showing concern and compassion for their friend throughout these ordeals. Since Maggie was such a success, I adopted Daisy Mae a few years ago, another dog from the shelter. The two get along very well and love to play together.

As we continue to visit the retirement home every Wednesday, it is rewarding to watch Maggie lift the spirits of the residents and staff. Residents who never talk to anyone talk to her; people who do not leave their rooms come out to see her. Even people suffering from depression, laugh and smile and talk to us. Some residents never have any visitors at all so Maggie is the one true friend they look forward to seeing every week.

I really hit the jackpot with Maggie. Some people can't understand how I could spend so much money on "just a dog," but I feel sad for them—sad that they were never fortunate enough to have a dog like my Maggie. When I think of how much love she has brought to me and others, I hate to imagine what we would have missed if I had put her to sleep. I believe that Maggie was heaven-sent. That voice murmured over and over again in my mind, "This girl has a purpose." And she certainly does.

But right now she is barking outside the backdoor, saying "It's time to take me and Daisy Mae for our long morning walk—hurry up!" You can tell who's the boss in this house!

LOUIS

—— Frances Pilot, Freelance medical writer ——

In 2001, Louis, then called Loopy, was languishing in a back hospital ward at the New York City Center for Animal Care and Control (CACC). The puppy had various medical problems and was a prime candidate for euthanasia. In those days less than 1 percent of dogs in similar circumstances at the CACC survived, but it was Louis's lucky day. Sharon Malloy, CACC director of rescue, telephoned Marilyn Teres-Cavanaugh, director of NY Pet-I-Care, because she believed this dog might be the perfect Jack Russell terrier mix for me. I had been looking for a small, preferably female, poodle or terrier mix.

When I saw Louis, I was horrified. He was a dehydrated skeleton with a bad respiratory infection and other health issues. I adopted him immediately, and in return, he started to recover. As soon as he got settled, he began gaining weight at the rate of eight pounds a month and astonished everyone by becoming the world's first standard Jack Russell weighing in at 70 pounds! A recent DNA test showed that he is in fact 25 percent Doberman and 25 percent German shepherd; the remaining 50 percent of his DNA is too mongrelized to be identified.

Louis is a gentle giant, a wonderful, intelligent, compassionate therapy dog. He works at St. Vincent's Catholic Medical Center in Manhattan, the hospital that pioneered the first therapy dog program in New York City. Studies show that animal-assisted therapy benefits patients by lowering blood pressure, shortening hospital stays, and lessening the severity of pain. Today most major hospitals in New York have their own pet therapy programs; St. Vincent's was the trailblazer.

Some of Louis's greatest successes have been with neurology and oncology patients. Despite his size, he has always specialized in bed visits. For six weeks he visited a patient with ovarian cancer who missed her own large dog very much. Louis lay on a clean sheet on the bed; together they enjoyed cuddle sessions of an hour or more during which the patient was able to delay her pain medication. Another time we were assigned to a young woman with a serious heart condition. She had been separated from her three dogs for months. When Louis jumped onto her bed, she began to pet him and immediately burst into tears. I was worried that Louis might have hurt her somehow, but she explained that she missed her own dogs and was terribly afraid that she might never see them again. Louis gave her a chance to share some of her feelings. While he can't perform miracles, he certainly has improved the hospital stays of many patients.

He has helped people recovering from stroke and brain injury. On Christmas Day several years ago, he helped a stroke patient learn to move his fingers again. Louis loves to be scratched under his chin, and he simply would not give up nudging the man's hands until he responded.

Louis is more effective than flash cards for helping patients recall language and memory: He often reminds people about dogs from their past. He walks patiently beside wheelchairs and participates in group physical therapy sessions. He loves to visit pediatric patients and enjoys babies who stand and peer at him from their cribs, like small humans in a zoo. Louis plays with older children with cystic fibrosis, helps rouse children post-anesthesia, and motivates children to start moving after surgery. He also visits hearing impaired and blind patients: Sitting recently with a blind patient and her two blind visitors, he enjoyed their tactile approach to visualizing him.

Louis has also formed close bonds with hospital staff, in particular with the nurse on the orthopedic floor who feeds him roast beef sandwiches. He insists on stopping there for lunch prior to work. Most of all, he likes to visit Edna Wolf, coordinator of the pet therapy program at St. Vincent's. He loves her for herself, of course, but her office also happens to be a giant playpen for dogs, filled with toys and treats.

Louis is perfect proof that sick shelter animals should not be considered damaged goods.

SERENA

—— *Steve Briggs, Pet therapy evangelist,*
recently converted horseman, restauranteur ——

Before Serena came into my life, I had a beloved Australian shepherd who was with me for eleven years; by the time she died we had hiked over 6,500 miles together. A year later I tried to rescue another Aussie, but that attempt failed. With the help of a professional trainer, I worked with the dog for six weeks but she was just too wounded emotionally. She loved me, but ended up biting my wife, Doris; Max, our Tibetan terrier; and finally the Florida Power and Light lady. I was pretty devastated when I had to give up on her.

That spring Doris and I headed north with Max and our two Paso Fino horses. Along the way we stopped to ride for a week in Aiken, South Carolina. My wife saw an ad in a local paper for an Aussie being fostered by Molly's Militia in Augusta, Georgia. We looked at their Web site and there was Serena, certainly not an Australian shepherd but very appealing. Doris was intrigued by the name they had given her—Serenity. The dog was picked up as a stray when she was about three. She had been living on the streets for several months and had had a litter of puppies. She was in pretty dismal shape. Molly's Militia

had rescued her from animal control where they were putting down roughly 1,000 dogs each month.

Doris and I drove to Augusta to see Serena at her foster home. She was timid and shy but her eyes and her demeanor were kind and beguiling. She and Max got along well so we took her back to Aiken with us. That evening we went to a restaurant with an outside dining terrace. Max has extremely good restaurant manners, and Serena simply lay down next to him under our table, just as if she knew exactly what to do when going out for dinner.

Two days later, Doris and I, with Serena, Max, and our two horses, moved on to West Virginia to ride in the mountains for a week. There, we let Serena off her lead and found that she was happy to follow us everywhere. She loved going with the horses and always stayed near us. We knew that she was meant to be part of our family.

We continued north to spend the summer in New Hampshire. I probably should mention that the only problem this dog had was a tendency to get carsick. In November we returned to Florida; in January I started training Serena for therapy work. Soon we

received certification from the Delta Society with a complex rating. This rating means that dog and handler are qualified to work in highly active environments with many distractions and can work in situations that have a high degree of unanticipated interactions. Basically this means that Serena has the temperament, discipline, and calmness necessary in dealing with abused children and patients with dementia, as well as in other situations that might upset the average therapy dog.

We have worked at the Naples Community Hospital and at several nursing homes. It has been a moving and rewarding experience. One day I watched a patient's blood pressure decrease as he petted Serena. I knew that there were studies showing this effect, but it is extraordinary to actually watch it happen. On many visits we heard patients say, "This is the best thing that has happened to me since I came here." One lady suffering from dementia carried on a conversation with Serena for five or six minutes; the nurse said that this was the most sense the woman had made in a long time.

On one visit, Serena absolutely refused to leave a patient's room and I finally had to almost drag her out. On our next visit, the head nurse told me that five minutes after we left they had a Code Blue and lost the patient. Another time, a man couldn't quite reach Serena from his horizontal position, so he patted the bed to get her to come a little closer. The next thing I knew we had an airborne fifty-two-pound dog about to land on the chest of a man who was recovering from triple bypass surgery. I managed to catch her in mid-air. It was pretty exciting!

Through our local humane society we visited with a dozen kids from a residential facility. All of them came from difficult homes, and many had been abused. At first they avoided my big black dog like the plague. It took almost twenty minutes, and one very brave boy, but Serena eventually had five kids crawling all over her. She loved it, and they did too.

When we are in South Carolina, we visit a Veteran's Administration hospital and the Medical College of Georgia Hospital in Augusta. In addition, we visit a child advocacy facility where children who have been abused are interviewed and evaluated.

Serena helps put them at ease and makes it easier for them to talk with the authorities. The children create wonderful drawings for her—a bonus souvenir. We also work in a reading program at a special daycare center for at-risk children.

I'm no longer doing long-distance hikes so I guess God decided that I needed a dog with another mission, one that brings joy and smiles to people who need a little cheer in their day. The amazing thing is that I hate hospitals and am terrified of illness. In 1976 I was diagnosed with cancer and told that I had six months to live; ten years later I had a recurrence. It wasn't easy but since Serena is so special and most of the people we visit are so moved and so appreciative, I find that I barely notice the serious illness that grips many of them. I'm determined that Serena and I will be the best therapy team we can possibly be.

MANDY

—— *Karen Mangini, Fitting model/design consultant* ——

Several years ago, I went to an animal shelter looking for a cat, but I was heart-struck by a mangy little brown dog. There was a large, red check mark on her cage; meaning she would be put down later that day. She had been returned to the shelter three times for being feisty and not good with children ("nippy" was the word they used) and was considered unadoptable.

I had no idea what I was doing. I had never had a dog before, but I felt compelled to rescue her. On the way home this skinny

little mess tried to bite me. I snapped back at her and instinctively grabbed the back of her neck. She settled right down. Maybe she remembered her mother enforcing a lesson in manners.

Mandy turned out to be a purebred cocker spaniel. She does whatever I ask: She sneezes on command, dances, and even prays. My secret? I hold an image in my mind of what I want her to do and project this image to her. After much time, love, and a great deal of patience, Mandy received her therapy dog certification. She is now a wonderful little love dog who opens everyone's heart and helps people heal.

At first we were affiliated with an organization that supervised pet visits at a large children's hospital. Mandy got fired from this organization for praying—yes, praying. (It's just an endearing trick: She sits, places her paws against my arm or a pillow, then puts her nose down on her paws to "say her prayers.") Apparently there had been a person working with this organization who had her dog "pray" for patients, then proceeded to try to convert them. The organization was forced to make a rule—no praying! Well, we complied for a while but then I began to feel it was silly. Many patients wanted Mandy to pray for them. After all, she has no agenda, and I don't either, so she prayed, and after the third reprimand, they let us go.

We certified with another organization and now Mandy prays whenever anyone asks her to. We visit hospitals and the Lull Special Education Center. Several times we visited a man who was in a coma, and when he regained consciousness the only thing he remembered was Mandy's name. At Lull we visited with a child who had been almost totally unresponsive for months. I didn't realize this and was not surprised when the child showed interest, even delight, in Mandy and her antics, but the teachers were amazed at the change in this child.

Mandy loves coming to Lull, a school that serves students ages three to twenty-two with a variety of disabilities including autism, hearing and visual impairment, and significant developmental delays. Sometimes, wearing her pink tutu, she likes to dance and do tricks for the children. Occasionally some of them may be a little afraid of dogs but they get over it quickly. The teachers say that it is especially important for these children to learn to be comfortable with dogs because some of them may need a guide or service dog in the future. Mandy usually knows what the kids need; she likes to interact with them but always stays a safe distance from the ones who want to grab her soft furry ears.

Mandy and I are kindred spirits. I was almost made a ward of the court when I was fifteen, but with a chip on my shoulder after abuse by multiple family members, I ran away from home instead. No one admitted to the abuse until years later. No one took the time to understand me. Mandy had been repeatedly rejected and returned to the shelter. No one had taken the time to understand her, either.

I hope my story can inspire other victims of abuse to realize that they are not alone, that they can let go of the past, move on, and heal. I never knew what love was until I met Mandy, who truly opened my heart. She was the first being I felt safe to love. Mandy was brought to me so that I could know what it means to have an open heart; so that I could know what it means to love. We both needed love, guidance, and purpose. We found it in each other.

PECOS

—— Lestia Bopp, Semi-retired adventurer ——

One day, driving into town from my cabin in the mountains, I spotted a dog by the side of the road. He was standing on a boulder, howling toward town many miles below. He looked like a herding dog and may have fallen from a sheep herder's pickup. He was very skinny but muscular and work-hardened. He was so fearful that it took a long time and some struggling to get him into my car, but he never once showed any inclination to bite. He had a nasty gash on his leg so we went straight to the vet's. Again I was impressed by the dog's gentleness as the vet cleaned out the wound and sewed up his leg.

I gave him a name, Pecos, but nice as he was I knew I couldn't keep him. I had a very active outdoor life centered on long-distance horseback riding. Sometimes I would be out for days, sometimes weeks, and I loved the opportunity to see wild animals who often are not afraid of a horse, but I thought a dog would be a different story. I put ads on the radio and in the papers, called the shelter and all the vets, even contacted the forest service about sheep ranchers with summer grazing in the area, but no luck.

I was determined to find him a good home because he seemed like such a good dog. Eventually a friend agreed to take him, but when I brought him over to her house he walked in and immediately peed on a plant near the front door, something he had never done before. He certainly ruined that deal. It was as if he had realized that he might end up somewhere else. He had chosen me, and that was that.

Two years later I had a terrible mountain biking accident. The handlebar smashed into my right eye, basically exploding it. I already had a damaged cornea in my left eye leaving it with only about twenty percent vision. Before the accident, *that* had been my bad eye; now it was my only eye. The accident also injured my brain, affecting my equilibrium. I spent the next two months going from one hospital to another. After three lengthy and painful operations, the doctors told me there was no hope; none of their efforts could restore my vision or relieve the pain and pressure inside my head. I realized that my active and adventurous life was over, and I sank into a deadly depression. I wanted to die. At one point in the hospital my heart simply stopped, and I felt absolutely no gratitude or happiness when I learned later that I had been resuscitated.

Finally back at home, I spent weeks bedridden, in horrendous pain, unable to walk, confused, and despairing. All the while Pecos stayed at my side, occasionally licking and nuzzling me, sometimes whining in a way that seemed to say, "I love you, please get better." He understood I was really in

trouble. When friends came by to bring food and take Pecos out, he was always reluctant to leave me.

When I started to try to walk again, he glued himself to my lower leg, nudging me away from objects I could trip over or stairs I might tumble down. When I took a walk outside for the first time, he yipped in excitement and did a gleeful little dance around me. Then he resumed his position at my side; we both knew that he had made it his mission to encourage me and to guide me.

At first he herded me around, always in contact with my leg. He would nudge me away from the stairs, then if I seemed determined to go down, he would stand in front of me until I got a good grip on the railing. I bought a guide dog harness for him, but at first he didn't like it. He wanted to do the job his own way, his herding way. Still, it only took two or three days to get him to accept the harness and a different way of guiding— leading me instead of herding me. He adjusted his pace to mine, and he learned to avoid uneven footing where I might stumble. He's so intelligent that he figures out a lot on his own. I did have to teach him not to lead me under low hanging branches. After a collision, I would show him the branch, maybe shake it a little, and in only a few days he realized that we had to go around these things even though they posed no problem for him alone.

I have been very lucky with Pecos: He quickly adjusted to life as a service dog. But no one should think he can train his own guide dog. It's too risky. I have had valuable help from dog trainers, especially in teaching Pecos to guide me safely on the street. Professional help has made a huge difference.

I live in a small town where many people are kind and helpful, but the general public needs to learn more about service dogs. Today many people realize that they should ask permission before approaching a dog that is working. Loose dogs are a more serious problem. Many dog owners here allow their dogs to roam around town with no leash, and sometimes even with no owner. Pecos doesn't like it when another dog gets in his face. And he's quite right. Once, when he was guiding me down some stairs in town, a dog rushed up out of nowhere and lunged at him. Pecos grabbed that dog by the nose so quickly I didn't know what was happening. Then the owner showed up furious. Her dog was loose, out of control, had attacked a working guide dog, and she was furious about a little blood on her dog's nose—amazing! It was a very dangerous situation, as I could easily have fallen down the stairs with both dogs.

Pecos has been welcomed everywhere we go, in stores, restaurants, and doctors' offices. We often ride the bus into town. On the street, he stops before every curb and waits for me to tell him to go forward. It's up to the handler to tell the dog when to cross, but even though I usually see the vague outlines of cars, I can't always tell how far away they are or how fast they're coming. Pecos will refuse to obey the forward command if I screw up and tell him to go when something is headed toward us. I call that intelligent disobedience.

This dog has kept me out of trouble of all kinds. Once, when we were going to a nearby trail for his daily off-leash run, he stopped and refused to go any further. I could tell there was a car some distance away with a person standing next to it, but the scene was pretty blurry. Pecos started to pull me in the other direction. I couldn't figure out what the problem was but nonetheless I turned obediently to follow him. Just then, I heard this very drunk male voice say, "Hey, baby, where are you going?" Somehow Pecos knew this was a hazard to be avoided.

Not long ago I had some trouble with my inner ear; sometimes I could hardly stand up or walk. Pecos seemed to know when these attacks were coming. One day in the waiting room at the doctor's office, I told him to follow the nurse. He refused and pulled me toward the sofa. I was embarrassed and a little annoyed so I insisted that he follow her. A few seconds later I had an attack and fell to the floor. I then realized that I needed to pay attention to him instead of always assuming that I know better.

Pecos's ability to sense danger and keep me out of harm's way helps me go out into the world knowing that I will be safe with him at my side. Without him I could be a miserable recluse, but with him beside me everywhere we go I feel like I'm being escorted by the canine version of George Clooney crossed with Jack Bauer. Does it get any better than that?

DIXON

—— Karen Kirchner, Associate producer ——

When I was a child my family had dachshunds, so a few years ago, looking for a dog of my own, I checked dachshund rescue groups online. I wanted a young dog, a small one, definitely a female. Then a representative from Gold Coast Dachshund Rescue called me to inquire, "May I introduce you to a dog I think you will like? He's a seven-year-old male, fairly large." Well, for once I got out of my own way. I agreed to see him.

For seven years Dixon had lived with someone who had no time for him. He was left alone in a backyard, not socialized with people or with other dogs. When I met him at Petco, he seemed withdrawn, not responsive at all, but he gave me a look that said, "I'm so scared. Please help me!" I couldn't turn away.

Dixon was not interested in humans, and he certainly didn't want anything to do with other dogs. How was I to start socializing him? Well, Petco gives a lifetime of training classes for any dog adopted through one of their locations, so it seemed logical to take him there for classes. During the first session he turned his back on the class and put his head between my ankles. By the next class he became comfortable enough to watch the other dogs, and by the end of the first course he even started to participate a little. Slowly he developed some dog skills; he learned to greet other dogs with a quick sniff at each end. He had no idea what to do with a toy, but since then he's come a long way. Now he opens the toy box himself, chooses one, and brings it over to engage me in play.

In addition to the classes, I went to great lengths (and some sacrifice) to socialize him. I patronized any restaurant regardless of the quality of the food as long as they allowed dogs on their outdoor patio. I always tried to sit near the entrance so everyone had to pass us. If people showed the slightest interest in Dixon, I invited them to pet him and offer him a treat, and slowly he began to equate humans with good things.

Somewhere around the end of our third stint in dog school—I think it was our twenty-third class—Dixon had a breakthrough. It was a Helen Keller moment. He suddenly realized that he could communicate with me, and that treats were involved. At first he used the down position to ask for everything: He would lie down in front of his bowl, by the front door, next to the couch. On a walk, if I went straight when

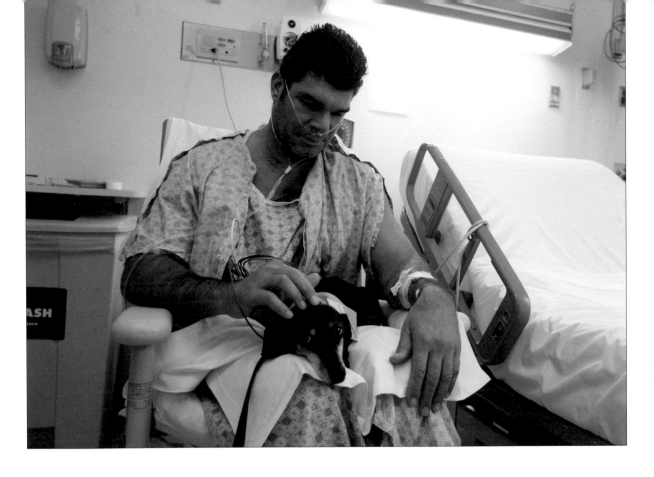

he wanted to turn onto a different street, he would stop and go into the down position facing the way he wanted to turn. Since I expected him to learn some of my language, I felt I should learn some of his. I read every book I could get my hands on about dog training and dog communication. I learned to send him calming signals by yawning or looking away. I learned to understand his signals, some common to all dogs, such as tail placement and movement or ear placement, but also some signals that seem specific to him. If he wants to be left alone when I am petting him or brushing him, he places his muzzle beneath the palm of my hand and pushes up. If he wants petting or attention, he comes over and places his muzzle on top of my hand pushing down. Our communication has just gotten better

and better, but I must admit that it took longer for me to catch on to his signals than it did for him to understand mine. As in any good relationship, we understand each other more and more as time goes by.

Later that year Dixon received his American Kennel Club Canine Good Citizen award, then after more training he was certified by the SPCA of Los Angeles and the Delta Society as a therapy dog. Because by then he was eight, there was some concern that he might be too old for the Delta program, but fortunately he was allowed to take the test, and I'm here to tell you that you absolutely *can* teach an old dog new tricks. Dixon is eleven now. He has a slight limp from femoral and pelvic fractures due to a mishap with a car long before I met him; he also has spinal inflammatory disease and epilepsy. But none of this slows him down, not even for a minute.

We currently visit patients at Cedars Sinai Hospital in Los Angeles and at Henry Mayo Memorial Hospital in Santa Clarita. At Cedars Sinai, a very dog-friendly place, we go to the cardiology ICU and the AIDS and cancer wards. In the hospitals Dixon has a cocky little walk; we call him Dr. D. He adapts his behavior to each patient: With the cardiology ICU patients he is very calm and quiet, and with the AIDS and cancer patients he's always ready to play if they're in the mood. Dixon was recently nominated for the Red Cross Hometown Hero Award. He and I received a Presidential Service Award for volunteer work.

I have had some heartwarming as well as heartbreaking experiences at the hospitals, but there is one experience that touched me deeply. On a Saturday afternoon Dixon and I went to the room of a young man I'll call Peter, who requested a therapy dog. When Peter saw Dixon, he seemed disappointed: He had wanted a bigger, fluffier dog. I offered to leave and get him signed up for the type of dog he preferred but he decided that Dixon would do in a pinch. When I put Dixon on the bed, Peter complained that he wasn't effervescent enough. Again I offered to leave, and again Peter said Dixon would do. At that point Peter's visitor asked if I would mind staying while he went to get a quick cup of coffee. After his friend left the room, Peter began to hallucinate and started to call Dixon "Rusty." (I learned later that Rusty was Peter's childhood dog, a golden retriever.) He said, "Rusty, I've missed you. Come to me, Rusty." Tears streamed down his face. Then Dixon did something I have never seen him do. He wriggled up Peter's side and buried his muzzle in Peter's armpit. The tears continued, but a smile appeared as well. "Rusty, you haven't forgotten. I love you, boy." Dixon started moving his muzzle around, tickling Peter. Peter let out loud wracking sobs mingled somehow with joy. "Rusty, you know what I like!" When Peter's visitor returned, Dixon and I left to visit our other patients. I could hear Peter talking to his memory of Rusty as we walked down the hallway. After we completed our visits, I decided to return to Peter's room. He was gone, his bed stripped. A nurse told me that Peter had passed away a few minutes after Dixon and I left. The sadness of seeing someone so young reach the end of his life broke my heart, but I knew that Dixon had helped Peter feel that he was leaving this world with his beloved Rusty at his side.

My regular job is a demanding one so I'm often tired by the weekend, but on Saturdays when Dixon and I go to one of the hospitals for our therapy work I always end up feeling energized. It's exciting and very gratifying to see the effect Dixon has on "his" patients.

CERES

—— JoAnn Craig, Retired professor ——

When he was only a six-month-old puppy, he was a throwaway dog. For more than a week he waited beside the highway, hoping that the people who had abandoned him would return. He was scared and hungry; he ate grass, leaves, and twigs. Finally, a lovely young lawyer named Kim and her kind husband spotted him and stopped their car. As soon as they opened the door the dog jumped right in. They went to the nearby town to ask if anyone had lost a dog. Several people said, "Is that the dog from up on the highway? We can't believe he's still alive. He's been there more than a week." No one had tried to help.

Kim took the puppy to Second Chance Rescue where my daughter Leslie, who has a dog grooming business, sometimes volunteers to wash and groom dogs to help them become more adoptable. Leslie liked the dog and thought he might be a good match for me (although at that point I didn't realize that I needed a dog).

I was lonely and sick, on a leave of absence from the University of San Francisco, trying to heal from lung cancer. To please Leslie I went over to Kim's house the next day to meet the dog. To my dismay I saw a very sad, ugly, and depressed dog. He looked weird: His head and feet were too

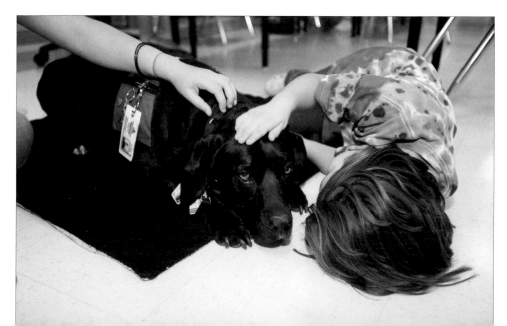

big for his body, which was way too skinny. Also, his head and feet were dark black and his body was reddish-brown. He was not playful; there seemed to be no fun in him. But Kim said, "This dog is faithful, loving, brave, and very intelligent." Then she told me his story.

When I thought it over, I knew that he was my dog, so I named him Ceres for Sirius the dog star and for Ceres, the largest asteroid in the asteroid belt. I took him home with me. On the way, we stopped at Leslie's shop. She gave Ceres a party on the spot to celebrate the first day of his new life. She gave him a fine blue bed, a ball, a bone, a bully stick, dishes for food and water, and a beautiful new red collar and leash with his own nametag. After we got home, I began to worry. After all, I had not had a dog for over thirty years. I think Ceres was worried and nervous too. I went straight to the library for books on dog training, and then signed us up for training classes.

It was astonishing—in less than two weeks Ceres changed from a depressed, listless, disheartened dog into a curious and joyful dog. He ate well, relishing his food, and he was bursting with energy. When Leslie came to see him, she was amazed. "I'm so sorry, Mom. I thought he was quiet. I hope he's not too much for you!" But I loved his playful personality. He and I were both lucky to be alive and to be together. He took me for walks, visits to parks and to dog school, and everywhere we went we met new friends. Ceres grew into his body and his coat turned a shiny black. The vet thinks he is part Labrador, part Great Dane. Wherever we go, people say, "What a beautiful dog!"

Ceres has very good manners. He knows the commands *sit, stay, heel, come, fetch, wait*, and, most important, *leave it!* He loves to do tricks like high five, shake hands, "kiss the lady's hand," take a bow; and he fetches a tissue when I sneeze. He also brings in the paper and the mail, carries bags from the store, picks up things that fall, and fetches my slippers when I'm tired.

I learned about animal-assisted therapy, and after some more work and study Ceres and I became a certified therapy dog team. Then I had my fingerprints taken so we could volunteer at the Valley of the Moon Children's Center. With Ceres' help I now spend the best part of my time and energy helping abandoned, abused, and neglected children. The students, ranging from ages six to eighteen, are at-risk kids waiting for foster care or other care. Many are from homes where the parents are involved in drugs, mostly crystal meth. Susie James, the head teacher, agreed to bring us in for pet therapy. She told me later she didn't expect much but thought it would be fun for the children to pet a nice dog.

On our first day, I gave a thirty-minute Power Point presentation about "Ceres the Throw-Away Dog," then for half an hour Ceres showed off his repertoire of tricks. Susie decided we could visit on a regular basis. In the beginning the lessons were somewhat random, about dog safety, dog behavior, and so on, but after a while Susie and I began to see how the lessons could reinforce the character-based values and life-skill ethics that the school was teaching the children. I worked with Susie to coordinate my presentations with the curriculum and its themes relating to building character, responsibility, respect, empathy, caring, and compassion. All this helps the traumatized children become healthy and responsible people.

Recently we went to the children's center for class. Ceres had been stung in his mouth by a wasp the evening before but seemed better that morning. However, by the time

I started the day's program he was acting subdued and depressed. He was obviously in pain and couldn't do anything but look dejected. He is always the one to cheer the children up, to make them laugh, to follow their instructions by doing tricks for them, but this time he was not able to help them. The children petted him and some began to perform the Tellington TTouch on him. These children—sad, betrayed, lonely, sometimes bitter and angry—realized that Ceres was in pain and rallied around him, showering him with love and compassion. As I watched, I began to see that all our hard work was actually succeeding. The children were learning to feel compassion and kindness again. Those who were not actually working on Ceres all seemed riveted to him by their tender expressions. After class everyone came up to pet him and talk to him. Witnessing their compassion was like seeing broken plants bloom after watering and tender care. It seemed like a miracle.

Ceres helps the children in many ways. One child said, "Sometimes I feel afraid, but when Ceres comes, he always makes us relax and feel happy. When Ceres makes a mistake, JoAnn never scolds him. She says, 'That's O.K., Ceres, you can do it. That's a do-over.'" The children love do-overs; they have become much more tolerant of each other's mistakes and problems. We teach them to treat animals humanely, and these lessons carry over into encouraging them to show caring and compassion for other human beings as well. When children have been traumatized by humans, they may sometimes need to learn to care deeply for animals before they can trust and care for humans again.

Six-year-old Joey did not feel very good about himself. Like many children, he thought that he had been sent to the children's center because he was "a bad boy." He ignored the teachers' attempts to reassure him. After his first class with Ceres and me, Joey wanted to pet Ceres. Another student volunteered to tell him about the three rules for proper and polite dog greeting. After Joey (1) asked permission of the owner (me), he then (2) asked permission of the dog by letting Ceres sniff his hand until Ceres stopped sniffing, then (3) Joey knelt by Ceres' side to pet him on the chest and neck. Ceres began to cover Joey's face and hands with kisses, something the dog had never done before. I said, "Joey, Ceres loves you so much. You must be a very good boy." "No," said Joey. "I am not a good boy. I am not good." I replied, "You are a good boy, Joey. Ceres knows, and he doesn't make mistakes about important things like that."

But Joey couldn't believe me, so he said, "Can we ask Ceres?" All the children know that Ceres can answer questions: one bark for no, two barks for yes, and three barks for maybe. Ceres has never once disappointed me by giving an inappropriate answer to any question from a child, and he refuses to answer private or mean questions. He is very good at reading body language, and even thoughts and feelings, so I was not worried that he might give the wrong answer to this critical question.

We asked Ceres, "Is Joey a really good boy?" And Ceres spoke up with a loud and clear voice, "*BARK-BARK!*" There was no mistaking what he said and how loudly he said it. Little Joey stood up tall and straight and swaggered off saying, "If Ceres says it's so, it must be true."

I gathered up my dog supplies and left the room choking back some tears. I saw a little boy's faith in himself restored by a brave therapy dog who had once been abandoned and abused, just like his friend Joey.

RITA

—— Robert Higa, Management consultant ——

When the time was finally right for me to adopt a dog, I knew what I wanted: a friendly, medium-sized dog, a good companion animal that would enjoy lots of outdoor activities and also be content to nap while I pursued my law school studies. After months of looking at all the local shelters, I came across Rita, a mixture of border collie, English setter, and Australian shepherd. She had been hit by a car and was recovering from surgery to repair a badly broken leg. Her owners couldn't afford to pay the thousands of dollars in vet bills, so they'd abandoned her at the animal hospital. As I watched Rita with staff at the Pets in Need shelter, I saw her charm and her ability to connect with people. Soon she was nuzzling up to me, and I knew that she was the dog I had been searching for.

Rita still had at least a year of rehab ahead, including follow-up surgery to remove several pins that were holding her front leg together. She now has a permanent bone plate and three screws. She was not allowed to put much stress on her healing leg so our activities were limited to on-leash walks, some basic obedience training, and simple indoor fetch-and-retrieve games. Her focus, ability, and willingness to learn were immediately evident. Once the leg was completely healed, we progressed from simple ball games to more complex activities, eventually competing at the top level in local canine Frisbee contests. Rita quickly mastered a couple of dozen commands while showing an ability to learn much more. Today she responds to over forty commands, many of which can be given either by voice or hand signals. She obeys even when the command is given by a complete stranger, or if a toddler tells her, "Sit!"

Rita's aptitude for Frisbee convinced me to have her try out for the Baseball Aquatic Retrieval Korps (BARK) team of water dogs sponsored by the San Francisco Giants and managed by Pets in Need. Dogs in BARK retrieve home run balls hit out of the stadium into the water at McCovey Cove. They work from boats, diving into the water on command, then they follow hand signals to locate and fetch the balls. After several months of training we made the team. Rita soon became team representative for media events and fund-raisers, promoting awareness of abandoned animals throughout the Bay Area. The publicity gained by the BARK team, especially during the Giants'

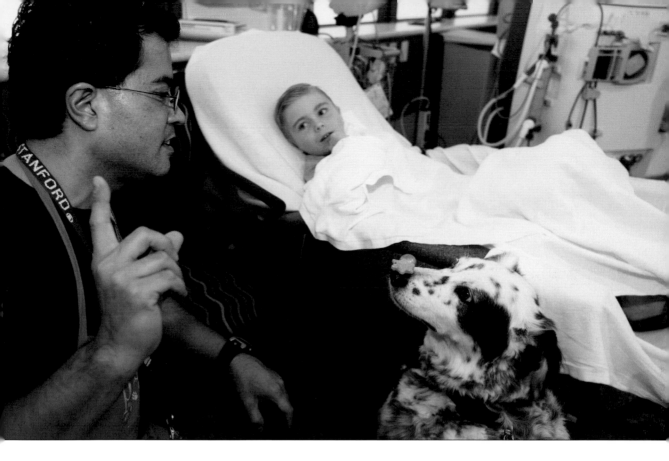

2002 World Series–season, contributed to record-setting fund-raising. Adoptions at Pets in Need more than doubled.

During our three years on the BARK team, I learned about pet therapy (animal-assisted activities [AAA] and animal-assisted therapy [AAT]) It seemed to me that Rita's wonderful temperament and her aptitude for doing tricks and entertaining people made her particularly well-suited for working with patients in hospitals. After a year of additional training we passed our first Delta Society evaluation in March of 2003. In 2005 we were accepted for PAWS, the pet-assisted wellness group at Stanford University Hospital and Clinics. With PAWS, we have paid regular visits to the medical/surgical unit, the physical and occupational therapy unit (PTOT), and the day hospital unit of the children's hospital (the Lucille Packard Children's Hospital at Stanford).

The PTOT sessions are always full of activity as we work with the staff to assist patients in many types of physical rehabilitation. On one typical day, we worked with a young stroke victim on regaining motor skills and learning to use a signboard to communicate. At first the patient simply petted Rita, great for motor skills and a pleasure for both. Then the patient became a little more animated and unsteadily but successfully pointed out letters on the signboard: T-R-I-C-K-S.

I explained a few of Rita's tricks and corresponding hand signals. With very limited motor function and no verbal capacity, but armed with a tasty dog biscuit in one hand, the patient managed somewhat abbreviated hand signals. The ever-motivated Rita connected with each one and responded flawlessly. I will never forget the look on that patient's face.

At the children's hospital day unit we visit with children receiving infusion therapy such as chemotherapy, blood work, and dialysis. Rita's tricks always bring smiles to the kids and provide relief and welcome diversion from their treatment. Some of the patients are Rita's "cuddle buddies," children who prefer cuddling and petting.

One day at the children's hospital we saw a little boy who was anxious to get to Rita. His mom put him down on the floor for a visit. He took a few steps holding her hand, then let go and continued walking the rest of the way to Rita. Once he reached us he started gently petting her on the head. I noticed that the mother was excited, waving at doctors, nurses, and therapy staff to watch as the boy stood steadily on his own, happily stroking the dog. I learned then that for months, ever since he had started treatments for an acute infection, the boy had not been strong enough or motivated enough to walk or stand on his own. I showed him how to balance a biscuit on Rita's nose and explained that she would wait for him to say "O.K." before tossing it up and catching it in her mouth. Rita got a large ration of biscuits that day.

It is tremendously satisfying to witness and participate—even in a small way—in a patient's recovery, but when our visits include patients who don't survive their illness, the magic of a happy, friendly dog can be especially meaningful. While I may get caught up in the emotion surrounding the plight of a sick child, Rita always seems capable of bringing out the best in any moment. Recently we visited lovely little three-year-old Ava who was tired and upset after a long day of tests and procedures. Ava immediately invited Rita to join her on the

bed and then called for a group hug with her mom, Rita, and me. At the end of our visit Ava thanked Rita with a gift of some precious fish artwork she had made herself. This was our final visit with Ava on one of the child's last remaining days. That day was made significantly brighter by the simple, heartfelt connection between a special kid and a special dog. An experience such as this confirms my belief that there is no better place for Rita and me.

Mary Delaney, charge nurse at the hospital, is one of Rita's fans. She says, "Rita distracts the children from the rigorous effects of chemotherapy and other invasive procedures. I see them smile and laugh as they watch her perform her amazing repertoire of tricks or settle down to snuggle with her. I see the anxiety on a parent's face disappear for a while when Rita and Robert enter a room."

In 2005, Rita and I assisted in the development and expansion of the visiting-animal program at Tony La Russa's Animal Rescue Foundation (ARF). I provided consultation and, with Rita, joined in as one of the founding therapy teams at ARF, where the Pet Hug Pack program today includes over eighty handler-animal teams visiting sixty-five facilities including schools, hospitals, adult day care, and rehab centers.

It has been a remarkable journey for both of us. As Rita relied on help and kindness from many human strangers, now she provides assistance and comfort to human patients. For me it has been an enriching and privileged experience to participate with Rita in these activities. Amid the stress, anxiety, and uncertainty of health crises, Rita and I are there for the sole purpose of providing pure and simple warmth and comfort in the form of four paws, a wet nose, and a wagging tail.

BLAISE

—— *Becky Stowe, Writer* ——

When my English springer spaniel, Jake, died, I went on a quest through the springer rescue network to find another. The challenge was finding a dog that could get along with Emma, the elderly springer now in charge of my home. I researched possibilities, some located very far away, but one day I got a call from the Columbia-Greene Humane Society more or less right in my own backyard. They had two nice male springers, a father and son. When the dogs' elderly owner died, her daughters didn't want to bother with them and simply turned them loose. Blaise and his dad, Brownie, were brought into the shelter as strays and spent several months there. I went over immediately to see them and liked them very much, so every day for the next two weeks I took Emma to the shelter to visit them. She finally agreed to let me adopt them.

Sadly, Brownie had stage-3 cancer and died after only a few months with us. Blaise was about seven and a little shy at first, but very sweet. I thought he would be good at therapy work so we started basic obedience training to prepare for the Good Dog Foundation (GDF) certification. Our trainer was Susan Fireman, GDF regional manager and executive trainer. Susan gave Blaise a temperament test to be sure that he would be comfortable and friendly with people and other dogs and that he would enjoy the work. The Good Dog Foundation provides volunteer teams with intensive training in both obedience and therapy work and then places the team in a suitable program. Our training for certification consisted of ten sessions to teach the dogs and their handlers the necessary skills and procedures to participate in animal-assisted therapy. As a volunteer I learned how to work with Blaise and also how to comfortably interact with all kinds of patient populations in a variety of situations. Blaise learned how to work with me to navigate in healthcare environments and to provide therapeutic assistance to people in need. When we completed the course, we were certified to work as a Good Dog Team. When we started making visits we were monitored and assisted; Good Dog requires recertification every year.

We visit the local hospital and Blaise's favorite place, the New Leaf Club, a program of the Mental Health Association of Columbia-Greene counties. The club's mission is to provide a harmonious and active environment for adults who are working on personal and vocational goals. Some people live in community housing, and some have their own apartments. Blaise, as a rescue, comes with a few flaws—only a few and only small ones (for example, he sometimes whines a little)—but his flaws are actually an asset at New Leaf. He is a constant reminder that one doesn't need to be perfect in order to succeed. His friendliness and his delight in performing (he loves to show off) more than make up for his little tics.

As soon as I open the door the room erupts with cries of "Blaise!" He makes the rounds greeting people, then jumps up on a chair at the table making everyone laugh as he looks around as if to say, "When does the party start?" Blaise is an icebreaker,

and people who are usually shy always have something to say to him. Some people just like to pet him, some like to toss him a biscuit, or watch him do obedience exercises or tricks. One of his New Leaf friends has discovered a skill she didn't know she had; she's taught him several new tricks. Another woman has overcome her fear of dogs. She had always watched Blaise from afar but was too afraid to interact with him. One day when Blaise was sitting at the table staring at the Trivial Pursuit board as if he wished someone would come play with him, she approached us and sat across the table from him. She told me why she was afraid of dogs and then asked if she could sit by him. When I said, "Of course," she moved over, sat down and began to touch him, slowly and tentatively. Her small hands trembled at first as she stroked him. "Good Blaise," she said. "Good Blaise." He sat there, patiently, and her face filled with happiness. "I love you, Blaise," she said. And Blaise loves everyone at New Leaf. The first day we visited there, a woman said, "Dogs just love you. They don't care what you look like or what you're wearing or whether you've had a bad day. They just love you."

In addition to therapy work Blaise and I compete in AKC Rally, a new sport that provides a stepping-stone from the Canine Good Citizen program to obedience and agility competition. Blaise recently achieved his Rally Novice title.

Competition is certainly fun, but the work that Blaise and I do at the hospital and at New Leaf is as therapeutic for me as it is for the people we serve. Without Blaise, it would never occur to me to visit strangers at the hospital or to sit quietly with a patient in hospice or to get to know some of the folks at the New Leaf Club. It's one thing to walk down a hospital corridor with a dog and stick your head in a door to say, "Hi! This is Blaise, the therapy dog. Would you like a visit?" It would be quite another thing to say, "Hi! I'm Becky. I'm a person. Would you like a visit?" Blaise gives comfort and love and makes people laugh with his tricks. People we visit tell me about pets they have at home, pets they had growing up, pets they have loved. Blaise's presence gives these people a little relief, a momentary respite from worry or pain, and I'm always amazed by how grateful they are. It's such a small thing that we do, but it gives such great joy.

SHADOW

—— Helen Chavez, Children's hospital administrative assistant ——

Shadow had a rough start. He was dumped in the Mojave Desert, then rescued and taken to an animal shelter. They put his picture on the Web site, Petfinder.com, where he was spotted by a woman who bred and loved border collies. She took him to her kennel, hoping to make him more adoptable. He stayed with her for a year. Being large and very timid around men, he was not easy to place.

I was looking for a small dog for therapy work and went to see Shadow. The woman who was fostering him said, "He's big, and you want a small dog. Everybody wants a small dog." He was nice, but he certainly was much larger than the dog I was looking for. I decided to go home and think it over. Next day the foster home woman called me. "The dog kept watching you yesterday as you left. Could you possibly foster him for a while? I think he'll do better in a home."

I thought, "Why not? At least I can do that much for the poor thing." I picked him up and brought him home in a brand new crate with a Laura Ashley quilt. After all he had been through I wanted him to have everything new. He did do well in my home. In fact he did so well that I never could let him go. I called him Shadow because he followed me everywhere. At first he was very fearful: If I picked up a brush, a broom, even a wooden spoon, he cowered and backed away. It was a year before he began to seem comfortable in my home, a year before he began to play with toys. My roommate's Pyrenees played with him and taught him about toys. The two ragdoll cats taught him about who's in charge. Shadow is a herding dog so it's not surprising that at first he tried to herd the cats. He has finally given up on that project. The cats will *not* be herded.

My friends were upset that I spent so much time with Shadow that first year, but I was working and could only give him my weekends. First he passed his Canine Good Citizen test, then we studied for the Pet Partners certification. The day of the test I was so nervous that of course my tension went right down the leash to Shadow, and he wouldn't walk with me. The evaluator suggested that we go out in the hall to practice where she could watch through a window. I became a little calmer, and he was fine. The evaluator said, "That's a good dog. He's always looking at you as if to say, 'What do you want me to do?'" And that good dog got his certification then and there.

During the past three years we have worked with cancer patients and others at Children's Hospital Los Angeles, the Shriners' Hospital, Hollywood Presbyterian Hospital, the psych unit at Verdugo Hills Hospital, a Ronald McDonald House, and the Arcadia Methodist Hospital. Everyone who meets Shadow loves him. He is calm and gentle and always seems to have a smile on his face. When I get his vest out before a visit, he dances around with excitement as if to say, "All right! Let's go!"

JADA, MARSHAL, and MARDI GRAS

—— Carl Massicot, CEO, Advanced K-9 Detectives ——

You may not know this, but the East Coast is in the middle of a bedbug epidemic. It's not so nice for people who find biting insects in their beds, but it's been a real business opportunity for me and my dogs. First, I started working with mold detection dogs; then we branched out into termites, until bedbugs began taking up all our time. We couldn't do it without the dogs. So far we have three dogs in K-9 Detectives. Jada, the small black mutt, was rescued from death row in an animal control facility. I think she may have been abused. She was pretty timid and fearful but she showed a strong play drive, which is useful for training dogs for all kinds of detection work. Dogs really don't care if it's bedbugs, toxic mold, cocaine, or explosives—they can learn to search for anything that has a scent. And because a dog's sense of smell is so sensitive, almost anything has enough scent for him to notice. A treat or playtime with a ball or a towel is the dog's reward, and that's what keeps him interested in working.

Marshal the black Labrador, also from a Florida pound, lives and works with my brother Ralph, and we have a beagle on the team, Mardi Gras. Mardi came from New Orleans, where she was rescued after Hurricane Katrina. Rescued dogs seem to want to work, or at least mine do. They love it.

We operate primarily around New York City and in the Boston area, but we also travel. Mardi fits under the seat in a plane, so it's easy for her to go along, but none of the dogs mind flying. Recently, we were in Texas and Florida, and I'm talking to people now in California and Las Vegas. The business is definitely growing.

We often work in hotels and apartment buildings, anywhere there's a problem, or, in the case of many hotels, places where they don't want to have a problem. I go into a room, let's say with Jada. I say, "Jada, seek!" She sniffs all around the room, and in two minutes she can tell me that the room is clean, or, if there are bedbugs present, she shows me exactly where they are. This makes it easy for the exterminator. Bedbugs are nocturnal and tiny, about one-eighth of an inch long. They hide in small crevices in walls, floors, beds, and other furniture. They can be almost impossible to find, unless you're a trained bedbug dog.

No one really knows why there is a surge in bedbugs in the United States, though increased international travel probably accounts for at least some of the problem.

A suitcase makes a good place to hide. A bedbug can live up to a year, and one female can lay five eggs a day. In six months, that's 5,900 bedbugs, and they're all breeding—and biting!

For twenty years I had my own construction business, but it was hard to get people to work. I even found guys asleep on the job. In those days I was always yelling. Working with the dogs is the best thing I've ever done. I'm a lot happier now that I don't have to yell anymore. In the morning when I say, "Does anybody want to go to work?" the dogs all rush to the door with their tails wagging.

BUDDY

—— *Jo-Ann Wagner, Clinical social worker* ——

My ten-year-old bichon frise, Buddy, was with his first owner for six years. She took him everywhere with her. He was fat and happy. But then he got very sick and lost most of his hair. The vet diagnosed him with diabetes, treatable with daily insulin shots. The owner insisted that he should be euthanized. It took a forty-five-minute discussion before the vet could persuade the woman to sign the dog over to her instead. Then the vet's husband and kids weren't thrilled, so Buddy moved in with the vet tech. Her terrier wasn't thrilled.

As I already had a bichon and had practice giving allergy shots to a dog, I figured insulin shots couldn't be very different, so I adopted Buddy. Since two of my dogs were certified therapy dogs I decided to train Buddy. He turned out to be a natural. And to think his owner would have killed him if she could have! Now he's my main working dog—a volunteer in many places, cotherapist in my child and family practice, and a HOPE Animal-Assisted Crisis Response dog. Two years ago we spent Christmas with Katrina survivors in New Orleans.

As cotherapist, Buddy is my welcoming committee, a pleasant surprise for a child coming to see a "talk doctor." He's a friend who likes you even if you have no friends. You must be special if Buddy is excited to see you, if he's wagging his tail and giving kisses. For the kids who come to my office, he's a constant—always there for them no matter what, always ready to give a dance or a high-five, always ready to get a smile. Children who have experienced trauma such as sexual abuse can tell Buddy what happened even when they may have been unable to verbalize it previously. A child psychologist in my practice actually refers patients to Buddy when they are too withdrawn to talk to anyone else.

Our volunteer work varies, from visiting with a patient in a hospital to disaster work with the American Red Cross and HOPE. We visited the grief-stricken Virginia Tech campus just days after the tragedy there. It seemed that every student, staffer, and visiting parent was happy to see Buddy approaching, ready for a pat and even a few tears on the top of his head, his tail always wagging. Trudging back to my van after that first difficult day, I saw what looked like a parking ticket on my windshield. I was relieved and happy to find a note from a grateful parent thanking Buddy and me for being there for their Hokies.

In fifteen years of volunteer work with four different dogs we have had the privilege and honor of several end-of-life visits. In one case Buddy and I visited a chemotherapy patient during his treatments. The man seemed to enjoy Buddy very much. He liked to stroke the dog's soft ears and talk quietly to him. One day a relative asked us to go see Buddy's friend at the hospital where he was now a hospice patient. We had a nice visit as we always did. I learned later that the man died shortly after we left. Buddy had brought him one of his last smiles on earth.

I always warn people not to get me started on the subject of therapy dogs, angels in fur. . . .

SOLEIL and MURPHY

—— Jason O'Neill, Professional ski patroller ——

When I was living in Colorado, I heard about a ski bum with a dog that had recently had puppies. He was anxious to find homes for them, so a friend and I went over to his apartment to have a look. As soon as we saw them we realized that they were much too young to leave their mother so we each chose one and agreed to come back in a few weeks to pick them up. When the time arrived and we couldn't reach the guy, we decided to go to his place. We discovered that he had simply moved out and abandoned the mother and the puppies. I took Soleil. She looks like small golden retriever, though her mother was a chow mix, and one of her sisters is black. She was a very active puppy. From the beginning we played hide-and-seek games. I would hide under the covers or in a closet. Sometimes I would step off the trail when she was busy sniffing a bush. Whenever she found me, I made a big fuss, praised her, and played with her.

I grew up skiing on a snow-covered garbage dump near Detroit, and was hooked on the sport even then. When Soleil was about a year old I was working on a ski patrol in Canada. I met a guy there who was active in canine search-and-rescue. He taught me about avalanche rescue. I liked the work, and Soleil turned out to be really good at it. She had the drive and the enthusiasm necessary for a successful search dog. For avalanche work, the dog begins to dig when he or she detects human scent in the snow. Either I or a friend of mine would hide in a snow cave with Soleil's favorite toy. When she found us, we would praise her to the skies and play tug with her toy. Sometimes we would bury a couple of dozen sweaters, boots, and mittens over an area the size of two football fields. It is all a big game to Soleil and she loves it. I now run the avalanche dog program at the Grand Targhee ski resort. We usually search one or two avalanches each year.

I can pick Soleil up and ski with her draped over my shoulders. She's perfectly relaxed even when I ski fast. It saves a lot of energy if she doesn't have to run through the snow. If I'm not around, Soleil will do a search in the snow for anyone on the ski patrol. She would probably do it for anyone who said, "Find it!"—and very likely she'd do it even without a verbal command.

Soleil had a great start, but I came close to wrecking her. She was a two-year-old avalanche dog. She had never done any other work when I took her to New York

City after September 11, 2001. We did urban search around the pile. There was so much stress, so much scent, and too much emotion. I shouldn't have been there, and Soleil shouldn't have been there. When we got home, she didn't eat. She slept a lot and lost a lot of hair. She showed signs of stress for several months but that winter we were back at a ski resort where searching and playing in the snow seemed to restore her energy and her drive. The next summer we started to train for wilderness area searches.

At first, someone would hold her while I ran away with her favorite toy and "hid" in plain sight. Gradually we made the searches more challenging, and she began to use her nose to find me and eventually to find other people, people who always had the favorite toy. She learned that she had to bring me to the person hiding before she got the toy and her game of tug. Whenever she thought we were going to search, she danced around me with excitement.

During the next winter, we were called out to search for a young snowboarder who had disappeared in an avalanche while riding alone on Teton Pass. We went out at 6 AM but it was too windy and dangerous to

proceed. By 9 AM they were throwing bombs to trigger slides and control the slope in the area where the man's tracks had been seen. At noon we began the search. We worked the slope for almost two hours. We were taking a break when Soleil suddenly got up and started moving. I could tell she had something. She just had that look. Then she lost the scent. She checked out a tree, the wind changed, and she turned, went about ten feet further and started digging hard. I skied by her to see if she would follow me but she was absolutely intent on that spot. We found the body right there under about four feet of snow and avalanche debris. Soleil was four. She had been working for three years. I was very proud of her. It was exciting to see her perform so well in a real situation.

Soleil also had a live find in a rural area. A woman attempted suicide with a drug overdose. She made a call on her cell phone, then wandered off. When we were called out, we did a building search at the house and moved into nearby pasture. It was a challenge: We were working in the dark, passing horses and deer. Soleil kept coming back to me to be sure I was following her. I would say, "Go back to work." Within ten minutes she found the woman alive.

When she was five, Soleil broke her back in a game of fetch. She spun in a way that blew up some discs between vertebrae. The swelling damaged her spinal cord. The injury was very serious, but she had major surgery that pretty much saved her life. She spent the summer swimming a lot, and by winter she was excited to get back to avalanche work even though she has a very slight limp. I had her recertified, and we were set to go again.

By the time Soleil was eight I thought she should slow down a little so I started to look for another dog. I found Murphy in the local pound. He's a large springer spaniel type, with hunting-dog energy. When I first saw him, he was jumping high in his cage, his head nearly reaching the top of the door with each leap. I thought to myself, "You could be a nightmare for someone who was looking for a nice house pet, but I think you'll be perfect for me!" Murphy's a rookie, but he certainly has great drive. He was certified last winter and he's been doing avalanche work for two seasons now. He's learning quickly. The Canadian Avalanche Rescue Dog Association (CARDA) holds a training course each winter. Although they take a very limited number of foreign dogs, Soleil qualified to go three times. I took Murphy last year and we will go again this winter. Murphy is also learning to do building searches.

Soleil still enjoys hunting for a buried boot in the snow, especially if she thinks she can get to it before Murphy can. The rest of the time she's happy to stay home with my wife, Charlotte. In fact she has become Charlotte's dog too. Often when Murphy and I are leaving early for work, Soleil will come down to have breakfast with us, then happily go back to bed when we leave. Charlotte's an important part of the team in many ways. She helps with training, and is understanding about the long hours and emergency callouts. It really makes a difference to have a partner like that.

LADDY

—— *Deborah Zapusek, Certified health-care provider* ——

Five years ago, an officer from Apache Junction Animal Control brought in a large Australian shepherd mix on the end of a catchpole. The dog was filthy, with matted fur, and was bleeding from the mouth. He was probably about eighteen months old. He lay on the floor panting, in a puddle of his own fear-induced drool. Working at the shelter as a volunteer, I saw the dog, and over the the next few days I spent time with him. The shelter was full, and one day when I came in I learned that he was on the eutha-

nasia schedule. I decided to pull him from the e-list to take him home and foster him until he became a little more adoptable. I thought he would surely make a good pet for someone.

In a very short time I realized what great qualities this dog had. He was patient, intelligent, and eager to please. He wanted nothing more than to be petted. And Laddy now had a name as well. I decided to keep him myself and train him as a therapy dog. He was certified five years ago. Together we visit an adult daycare center and an assisted living center. We are proud members of Gabriel's Angels, a therapy program for at-risk children. Laddy is an official mascot for Apache Junction Animal Control, the shelter where I found him. He gives back to the community he came from. He attends fund-raisers, parades, and even an occasional city council meeting. He recently passed a herding instinct test for the Arizona Herding Association.

In addition to all these achievements, Laddy worked hard with me to train as a service dog. He will retrieve almost anything. He can pick up a credit card on a tile floor or even a sheet of paper. He opens doors, brings in the newspaper, and can take off your socks without hurting your feet. He is trained to help stroke victims and people with arthritis, conditions that are prevalent in our family.

When Laddy and I visit the assisted living center, we always go to see Margaret, one of his favorite people. Before we arrive, Margaret, a retired dog trainer, hides dog treats all around her apartment and leaves her door ajar. As soon as the elevator door opens, I release Laddy, who makes a beeline for Margaret's door and pushes it open. After a quick sniff greeting for her, he circles the apartment picking up treats. In the unlikely event that he misses one, Margaret directs him with hand signals. Margaret reminisces about her dog training days when she actually achieved a CDX (a very advanced obedience rating) with a beagle—no mean feat. Laddy watches her as she talks, his tail wagging. Everybody's happy.

Through Gabriel's Angels and Citizens Against Family Abuse, we visit mothers and children at the safe house. When a recent survey asked children what they would miss most after leaving the safe house, many of them answered "Laddy!" I was volunteering at the Animal Control shelter when one of the safe house mothers came in. She recognized me from our visits, and said, "My three kids and I are getting a new home and one of the first things they want is a dog just like Laddy. Can you help me find one?"

Laddy, a dog no one wanted, has warmed many hearts over the years. He is living proof that great animals are out there waiting to be rescued and given a second chance.

TRIUMPH

—— *Moe Moeller, Retired executive director, American Red Cross;*
current volunteer ——

A Good Samaritan found Triumph bleeding by the side of a road in Turkey. Someone had cut off the husky's back legs and dumped her there to die. Triumph's rescuer took her to an animal shelter where a veterinarian treated her wounds and kept her alive instead of euthanizing her as many people would have done. Although this took

place in Turkey, it could have happened here in the United States. Cruelty to animals doesn't have a country.

In spite of the trauma she suffered, the dog was sweet and gentle, so as soon as her physical situation stabilized, the shelter set about trying to find her a home. There was a newspaper article about her, and people tried to spread the word, but after two months there was no one willing to take on an injured dog. Two shelter volunteers, Renin and her mom, Armagon, helped with Triumph's care and took a liking to the brave dog. They decided to reach out beyond the local area. They contacted Coral Isicki, a friend of theirs in Philadelphia. Coral put the story up on Siberian husky rescue sites on the Internet with a newspaper picture of Triumph, supported by a volunteer, while a veterinarian examines her mutilated legs. It's an image that's hard to ignore. When someone forwarded it to me, I read it until I came to the part about the dog being in Turkey. I thought, "What can I do about a dog in Turkey?" and promptly hit "delete." The next day another person sent me the same photo with the same message: "Can you please help this animal?" And I thought, "Maybe I had better pay attention here."

I joined forces with Coral and her friend, Belinda Manuli. After a six-week struggle, we managed to get a reservation for Triumph on Turkish Airlines. We gathered the necessary $500 from friends, relatives, and anyone who would listen. We wired the money to Renin and Armagon who arranged health certificates, a passport, and a travel crate for Triumph. Then at the very last minute when they were at the airport with the dog, Turkish Airlines told them that the costs had gone from $500 to $2100. I got an emergency call from Renin, and not knowing what else to do, I gave her

my credit card information. People in my office warned me that it could be a scam but I decided to go with my instincts. A few hours later Renin called to say that Triumph was on the plane. The airline however had refused to accept my credit card. The people there wanted cash, and Armagon, bless her heart, had gone to her life savings and put up the money, believing that I would pay her back, and of course I did—with a little help from my friends.

Triumph arrived at the Nashville airport late in the evening. I first noticed her blue eyes and the kind expression on her face, then saw the bones protruding from what was left of her hind legs. The wounds were infected. I took her home. First thing the next morning we went to my veterinarian.

For many years I had worked with severely abused dogs; dogs that had been damaged physically and emotionally. As you might imagine, Triumph required some intensive rehabilitation. In many ways we were in uncharted territory. Once the infection dissipated, I made pads for Triumph's stubs and for the first time since the injury she could stand and move rather than drag herself along on her belly as she had been doing. I was trained in Healing Touch and Reiki so I used some of those techniques. While I was working on her she sometimes licked my face, which seemed like a good sign. Triumph has a gentle, loving personality. When she arrived, I had four other dogs at my house, and I think they helped her feel at home. Everybody here plays nicely together.

At that time, there were no prostheses for dogs, but my friend, Tom Brady, who makes devices for humans, offered to make some for Triumph. When we first put the devices on Triumph she hesitated for a few seconds, but then took off running down the hall. It was as if she knew she had legs again. Tom and I were astounded and delighted. The new legs worked pretty well, enabling Triumph to get around at home, but when she played rough with the other dogs she sometimes pulled one off. Once, when another dog buried the device, Triumph stayed put right beside it. I could see her thinking, "I am not going to leave my leg!"

Some time later I heard about Dr. Robert Taylor in Denver, who had developed an implant process for prosthetic limbs. Dr. Taylor generously agreed to provide Triumph with permanent implants into which prosthetic legs could be placed. The legs are a great success but they slip on smooth surfaces and sometimes get in the way, so it's convenient to be able to remove them. Triumph was the first animal to undergo this procedure with important implications for human patients as well as for other dogs.

I felt that Triumph's friendly temperament and her disability made her a good candidate for pet therapy. We began working with Linda Brewer and Therapy Animals Reaching Clients (Therapy ARC). First there was an evaluation to be sure we were suitable. (Not all pets make good visiting animals; not all pets would even enjoy it.) With Linda's help I learned about pet therapy, and, with Triumph, prepared for the test: Dogs are put in a variety of situations to determine whether they will accept a friendly stranger, allow petting, or gently take an offered treat. Dogs must be calm around other animals and comfortable walking in a crowd. They must sit, lie down, and stay on command, and should be calm with exuberant or clumsy petting, restraining hugs, and even angry yelling. Handlers learn how to interact

with patients in many different situations. We worked hard and passed the big Delta Society test. We were duly certified with Therapy ARC. We then volunteered to visit at the Monroe Carell Jr. Children's Hospital at Vanderbilt.

On our visits, Triumph generally rides in a stroller or a red wagon like the ones used to carry children around the hospital. She can walk, of course, and sometimes she does a little, but the floors are slippery and the hallways are long.

The children, their family members, and the staff all seem to light up when they see Triumph. She's a smile-bringer. She just plain likes to visit and likes to be loved. The children enjoy stroking her soft fur and giving her animal crackers. Her sweet expression and that husky smile encourage them to reach out to her. Often I hear a parent or a staff member say, "That's the first time that child has smiled in the hospital." Visits with a friendly animal can make the hospital environment seem more normal; stress is reduced, and the healing process can speed up. I think Triumph was born to do this work. It's her mission in life.

Sometimes when we walk into a room, I can see Triumph focus on the person who needs her most. Once when we were in an airport, I noticed her zeroing in on a young man ahead of us. She just stared at him until he eventually turned around and asked, "May I pat your dog?" When I said, "Of course you may," he went down on his knees beside Triumph, petted her, then put his arms around her and wept. When he could speak again, he explained that he had recently returned from military duty in Iraq and that his own dog had died while he was away. Then he said, "You can't imagine how good it is to hold a dog."

ALLY

—— *Maureen Pranghofer, Inspirational speaker* ——

I have been more or less blind since birth. For many years I used guide dogs to help me get around. When my bone disease started getting worse I began to use a power wheelchair and had to give up my guide dog. It was a sad day for both of us. At that time, I was a graduate student at the University of Minnesota and had enough vision to wheel around in well-lit places. Several years later a freak accident left me totally blind. I spent a year at Blind Inc., where I learned to read Braille proficiently, to use a long, white cane, and to do household tasks such as cooking. I started my own business making Braille transcriptions and giving inspirational talks.

Then about ten years ago I was in an automobile accident that left me a functional quadriplegic. I have good use of my left hand and a little use of my right—I can't hold things with it but can type. After another year of rehab, this time for the quadriplegia, I wanted to use a guide dog again to help me navigate independently. The school in California where my previous guide dogs were trained sent someone to visit me in Minnesota to see if we could figure out a way for a guide dog to work with a wheelchair. Unfortunately, there were too many serious obstacles: It was impossible for me to know if the chair was lined up with the curb cut and no way to tell if the path ahead was wide enough for the dog and the chair. I continued to use my white cane for mobility.

A few years later I began to hear about service dogs. I applied to service dog training schools around the country but they all turned me down. The general consensus was that a totally blind person could not use a service dog—what if the dog picked up the wrong thing, something sharp? I was pretty discouraged until I heard about Hearing and Service Dogs of Minnesota (HSDM), right here in Minneapolis. I was afraid that they too would turn me down, but this group was willing to think outside the box. They had never trained a totally blind person to use an assistance dog but they were willing to give it a try. Two months later I met Ally.

Ally is a Labrador/golden retriever mix. She was in an overcrowded dog pound, and had very limited time to find a home. She had a pink collar and pink toenails, and she looked as if someone had taken pretty good care of her—who knows what happened? Kim, a trainer from HSDM, just happened to come to that shelter looking

for a small dog for a deaf person. Then she just happened to drop her car keys. When Ally immediately picked them up, Kim said, "Obviously, you need to be in the service dog program!" She signed Ally out for adoption and in the process learned that the four-year-old dog had been scheduled for euthanasia the next day.

Ally was eager to learn and did well in her basic training at HSDM. Then the trainer proceeded to work on specific ways in which the dog could help me. For instance, picking up my cane had been a challenge for me: When I stop the wheelchair, I put the cane down, but then I can't move forward until someone (or a good dog) gives it to me. Ally learned that task first.

Ally assists me in many ways: She retrieves anything I drop, carries things, and helps to pull off my jacket. Since I recently started using a walker in the house, she carries objects for me as we go from room to room. When a counter is too high for me to reach from my chair, she hands objects to a store clerk or a pouch to the teller at the bank. She opens doors in public places by pressing on the large push plate. We have one of these push plates on the back door at our house so Ally can let herself out into the fenced backyard.

One day Joann, my caregiver, brought her two golden retrievers with her when she came to my house. Ally and the visitors played happily outdoors for a while, then came inside. Ally settled down with me in the office, but the goldens wanted to go out, then to come in, then out again. Finally, exasperated, Joann said, "I am not opening that door again. You'll just have to stay inside for a while." A minute later Ally appeared and jumped up to press on the push plate; all three dogs went out to play. We just had to laugh.

Last summer I was knitting outside and dropped a needle. Not realizing that Ally had gone into the house with my husband, I called her. She heard me, ran through the house, opened the backdoor, and picked up the needle for me. It may not sound like a big deal, but her enthusiasm for work is really quite remarkable. I ask for her help many times each day, so we practice all the time, and of course she often gets treats as a reward. Ally likes activity—she loves to chase sunbeams or even flashlight beams, and pounce on them. I have written a children's book called *Ally's Busy Day: The Story of a Service Dog.*

I think Ally must know how much she means to me; she always wags her tail and seems happy to assist me even if it's just to put a crumpled piece of paper in the trash.

I keep pretty active speaking to groups, doing Braille transcriptions, and writing my inspirational songs. I like to sing and recently made a compact disc of my own songs. Always nearby, Ally has a lot of busy days; she helps me in so many ways. Best of all, she's a loyal, loving companion—a real sweetheart.

RUSTY

—— Sophie Craighead, Animal lover and advocate for the
human-animal bond ——

Rusty is a golden retriever mix. He was found chained to a trailer house, with his brother Lucky chained to a nearby boat on a trailer. They were five months old. Mary Ann Ahern, the saint of animal rescuers, spotted the dogs and stopped to offer a doghouse for them. The owner replied that they didn't need one—they could sleep under the tires. Mary Ann sent pictures around to various local animal lovers including me. I became obsessed with those two faces. I couldn't sleep and couldn't get them out

of my mind. We tried to buy the dogs, but the owner insisted at first that he would sell only Lucky; however when he realized that I would pay $50 apiece, he decided that Rusty could go with his brother.

We already had five dogs of our own so I planned to find them a good home. Well, within two days I knew they would never leave here. It was close to my birthday, which falls on the same day as our ten-year-old daughter, Sage's, so Sage said to her father, "Dad, I have an idea. Mom can give me Rusty for my birthday, and I'll give her Lucky for hers." Derek very sweetly agreed to this plan, and we promptly had a great birthday and puppy-welcoming celebration.

Rusty and Lucky were loving and adorable, as nice as could be, but they had never been inside a house before, so it was a challenge for them. At first they seemed to be scared of everything—slippery floors, stairs, the TV—but little by little they became accustomed to these things. They learned to trust us. Rusty seemed to have an easier time adjusting than Lucky did, but to this day both dogs will run to hide if they see a strange man in a baseball cap or hear the sound of a diesel truck.

For much of my life I have been interested in the bond between humans and animals. In my twenties when I lived in Washington, D.C., I joined People Animals Love (PAL), an organization whose mission is to bring humans and animals together. My dog and I visited the Washington Home for the Incurables. I soon became involved with Leo Bustad and a group of people who were providing pets such as fish, rabbits, and birds for forty inmates (many of them in for life) at Lorton Penitentiary. It was a challenging project, but the results were

exciting: There were very few disciplinary actions against these men once they got a pet. The warden was amazed. Through Leo, I became interested in the Delta Foundation, (later the Delta Society). Delta funded the first credible research on the importance of animals to people and specifically how animals affect health and well-being. I served on the Delta board for most of the next twenty years, acting as board chair for two years. For the past ten years I have served on the board of PetSmart Charities.

But let's get back to Rusty and Lucky. They were both so gentle that I decided to have them tested for therapy work when they were about two years old. Predictably, Lucky was afraid of wheelchairs and walkers, but Rusty was perfect. We joined Teton County PAL, the local Delta Pet Partner affiliate. Every Thursday we visit second-graders in an English as a second language (ESL) class. If the students reach a certain place in their reading by Wednesday, they get to read to Rusty on Thursday. Rusty loves the children. He listens patiently while they read to him and carefully show him the pictures. And the children love him. One day we were greeted by a little girl— let's call her Bianca. Bianca had on a glamorous purple satin dress with a boa and purple sandals with stacked heels. I said, "Bianca, you look beautiful. Are you going to a party?" Bianca replied, "I'm dressed up like this because today I'm going to read to Rusty!"

Rusty and I participate in a reading program at the local library, and we have also worked in a special education class. Rusty is the gentlest of dog souls. In a long life with many wonderful dogs, I have never known a sweeter one.

HOPE

*—— Sarah Willis, Volunteer coordinator for Catawba Valley
Palliative Care Center and Hospice ——*

The stray cat was raising her kittens near a house where a kind woman put out food for her every day. One day this woman's daughter was horrified to see the little cat covered with blood and struggling to drag herself across the road with a tiny kitten in her mouth. Using just her front legs, she had apparently crawled back and forth until all the kittens were safe under a nearby house. The woman who spotted the cat called the Humane Society of Catawba County. When she was finally safe at the

shelter, the mother cat continued to nurse and groom the kittens despite her horrible injuries. Her back legs and her tail were torn up, and she was severely dehydrated. The Humane Society is a small, rural shelter with no funds for expensive surgery, but the executive director, Rosalie De Fini, and volunteer June Robison were impressed by the brave mother and were determined to save her. Hope seemed like a good name for this cat.

Dr. Bruce Carlton at the Catawba Valley Animal Hospital agreed to amputate the cat's rear legs and part of her tail. Dr. Carlton thinks that she had probably gotten tangled up in the fan belt of a car. After the surgery, June Robison fostered Hope with her kittens. While Hope was recuperating, she crawled around June's house on her front legs. She even figured out how to use the litter box.

After all the publicity about Hope, the Humane Society managed to raise $4,000 to help with her medical bills. Thanks to Dr. Carlton's generosity, Hope's expenses were just $400, so the Humane Society started the Hope Fund for emergency medical treatment for shelter animals.

When I saw Hope's story on the front page of our newspaper, I called to ask about adopting her. At that point there were already fifteen people on a waiting list for her, and the plan was to wait another two months since she needed additional surgery. I added my name to the list and by the time Hope was ready, everyone ahead of me on the list had reconsidered. The people who didn't take her have no idea what they missed. She is such a joy!

Hope has become an excellent mascot and fund-raiser for the Humane Society. She goes to all their events and loves being a star.

She has become very social and seeks attention, even from strangers, which is pretty unusual for a cat. I was already doing pet therapy work at our local hospital with my Labrador, and I thought that Hope could be an inspiration to patients who were having difficulty adjusting to the loss of a limb. Things didn't work out at the hospital but the volunteer coordinator at hospice tracked me down and Hope and I became hospice volunteers. Hope's certification was not difficult because she had been handled so much during her recuperation, and she was just so sociable. She thought the certification test was simply another social event, another opportunity to be petted.

She "works" for our local hospice visiting people at the facility as well as some patients in their homes. Hope's first hospice patient was a woman who wanted a cat of her own but felt that her condition made it unfair to adopt one. She contacted our local hospice group and requested a cat visit. In this area Hope is the only cat certified for pet visits so we went to the patient's home. Hope lay on the bed and purred while the woman stroked her and talked to her. She was focused on Hope through the whole visit—I was only the driver! After that we visited every week. The patient and Hope really bonded. She insisted that I bring Hope to her birthday party, and even though there were many other guests she made Hope the center of attention, bragging about what a wonderful cat she is and telling everyone how much Hope means to her.

Hope likes everyone but she especially likes kids. She works with schoolchildren in the local Reading Education Assistance Dogs (READ) program though she thinks it really should be called Reading Education Assistance Cats.

ROXY

—— June Clifton, Retired nurse ——

From my wheelchair at the window I watched a van screech to a stop outside my house. As the door opened a dog jumped out and took off running down the street. Then the driver climbed out yelling. I guess the dog had vomited in the vehicle, and the man was furious. I went outside and told him I'd like to see the dog. I had already decided there was no way she was going back with that guy. When she finally returned, shaking and scared, it wasn't too hard to talk him into leaving her with me. He didn't like her, didn't want her, and he was still disgusted about the mess in the van. Roxy and I were happy to see him drive away.

I felt that I had to take her, but to be honest, I don't know what I was thinking. I had considered getting a service dog to help me, but this dog really wasn't a very good candidate. She was terrified of everything. She had never been around people except for the ones who raised her, and I don't think they were particularly nice to her. She had never been in a house before so she paced and panted. I guess she felt trapped. She tried to escape several times. Once she attempted to go through the window but she got stuck in the blinds. Another time she jumped over a high fence in the backyard. We went through three sets of obedience classes before she calmed down and got some confidence. I had heard about Happy Tails, a program that helps people with disabilities learn the skills they need to train their own service dogs. I met Joyce Weber, the amazing woman who started Happy Tails ten years ago. Joyce is a counselor who helps people with disabilities learn skills for living with greater independence. She always says that her background is in rehab, not in dogs, but she certainly has figured out how to use dogs to help people live better.

Roxy and I entered the Happy Tails program and went to classes where I learned how Roxy could help me. The other students and I learned how to navigate in public with a service dog. We learned that the Federal Disabilities Act requires that service dogs must be permitted access in public areas such as stores, restaurants, buses, and planes. After Roxy passed her Canine Good Citizen and Public Access tests, she got her in-service training cape. From then on, everywhere we went, people knew she was a service dog in

training. As part of the training process, we went out with other students and their dogs to various public places. Roxy and I attended classes every Saturday and Joyce, the hardest worker I know, was always there. She says she hasn't had a Saturday off for ten years, and I believe her!

After fifteen months, Roxy and I passed the service dog certification test. She's a big help to me. She picks up things that I drop, and goes to the refrigerator and gets me a Coke. She's good at opening containers; if she drops the lid, she picks it up. She can even open doors. She goes everywhere with me. I try to get out at least once a day. Often we go to the mall. Everybody there knows Roxy. She's a good dog and good company. I don't know what I would do without her.

MAJIK

—— Chrys Armijo, Student Web designer ——

When he was just an eight-month-old puppy, Majik's owners gave him up for adoption because they had too many pets. I was looking for a dog at the time. When I went to the Humane Society, I noticed someone walking this unruly puppy that looked like a handful. The minute he saw me he made a beeline across the room to sit down directly in front of me. He just sat there and looked up at me. I could tell he was smart so I adopted him. We started immediately at PetSmart obedience classes. Majik did great—he's always been intelligent, obedient, and calm, qualities the training reinforced.

My parents wanted me to join Happy Tails, a program that teaches people with disabilities how to train their dogs to help out. My parents thought a service dog could help me live on my own and be independent if by some chance or reason my health started going downhill. Majik had already shown me that he was capable of achieving much more than basic puppy training. I could see his intelligence, the excitement in his eyes, and his willingness to please, so I figured it couldn't hurt to give it a try. As it turned out, it was challenging for me to get started with the group. I have spina bifida, and I suffer from depression. Sometimes I get angry and frustrated easily, but I realized pretty quickly that you can't do that and train an animal. I found out that I had to understand that I was O.K. if I wanted to teach Majik.

We went to classes once a week for eighteen months, and as time progressed, I realized that joining Happy Tails had been a good decision. Majik learned to pick up things for me and to open doors. He can put his paws on my shoulders and lean his head down to give me a hug. He goes to school with me. We've got a huge connection. He's almost like my son.

I'm 100 percent independent so I don't need a dog, and I never wanted a service dog, but then I thought, "What's the worst thing that could happen? I would still have a good dog."

And yes, the parents were right on this one!

GRACE

—— *Cyd Cross, Animal behaviorist* ——

Grace spent the first two years of her life tied to a tow chain in some guy's backyard. During that time she had at least one litter of puppies. She was involved in organized dogfights where one of her ears was ripped completely off and the other partly severed. She has numerous scars on her head and front legs. Fortunately, there was a raid, and Grace and the other dogs were taken to a shelter. After three months there, she was facing euthanasia, but the staff liked her and managed to move her to another shelter, where once more she eventually ran out of time. The staff there also liked her (she's pretty irresistible); they managed to move her to yet another shelter where she spent eight months.

I worked for many years with Out of the Pits, a pit bull rescue organization. Alexis, my beloved pit bull ambassador, had died recently. When word got out that I was looking for a replacement, the people at Grace's shelter begged me to look at her. I wanted a rough-looking dog for my work, and her injuries and scars tell a compelling story. I wanted a dog that had been used in fights to help me explain that dogs should be considered individuals. They should not be routinely killed (as they are in many

shelters) simply because they have come from a dogfighting situation and because they are pit bulls.

Grace's friendliness was impressive. For my work in schools, I need a dog that is comfortable and solid around kids, a dog that can be patient while I'm talking. I took Grace home and soon discovered that she had an advanced case of heartworm, badly infected ears, and a tumor that was difficult to access surgically, but which, by the grace of God, the vet managed to remove. On top of everything, Grace was seriously overweight thanks to a well-meaning shelter volunteer who used to sit in the cage with her and feed her endless treats. She's still on a diet, but all the other issues have been resolved and we are moving ahead with her training by leaps and bounds—not to mention sits and stays! She passed her Canine Good Citizen test and she just recently received her Therapy Dog International certification. She accomplished all this in just one year and one month from the time I got her. Pretty impressive, especially when you consider the time she spent recovering from health problems.

Grace is sweet and outgoing. She attracts people wherever we go. Since everyone wants to pet her, she believes that is the reason she exists. She is my official working partner for humane education. I teach children about safe ways to interact with dogs and about how to treat animals. We talk about empathy and compassion, about the responsibility involved when you have a dog or a cat. We talk about spaying and neutering, and what to do if you see animals being neglected or abused. We talk about dogfighting. I want people to see the true nature of a pit bull.

Your greatest risk with Grace is being licked. When anyone pets her, she automatically wants to respond with a very quick kiss. Grace is an effective teaching tool. She gets the kids' attention and makes our lessons both meaningful and memorable. And they love her! Who wouldn't?

EINSTEIN

—— *Dr. Larry Myers, Professor of veterinary medicine* ——

With a colleague, Bob Gordon, I have completed a study using dogs to detect mammary cancer and prostate cancer. The results are promising but much more testing needs to be done. There has been entirely too much hokum in the media about cancer detection. However, I do think it's possible. Recently we saw encouraging results from a study in Britain with dogs identifying bladder cancer from urine samples. It's fun to train the dogs, but we need more testing. We need blind and double-blind tests. You

can have a strong feeling about the likelihood of dogs identifying cancer, but science requires that you prove it.

For our study, we adopted dogs from a local shelter. The dogs lived with various people. Volunteers under tight control trained the dogs to detect and alert us to cancer samples by sitting in front of the correct specimen. Once the study was completed, we found homes for all the dogs, except one, Einstein, named because she was without a doubt the dumbest dog I have ever known. When I couldn't find anyone to adopt her, she came home with me; she lived to be twenty. She may not have been smart, but she certainly knew how to enjoy life—perhaps not so stupid after all.

I have trained dogs for detection work in many different applications. I have provided dogs for fish farms, where they detect chemicals in the water that could be harmful to fish. I trained dogs to detect heat cycles in cattle and the dogs were just as effective as a bull in identifying a cow in heat, and much easier to house. As a result of that project, I was interviewed for an article in *Playboy* magazine—my first, and probably last, appearance in that publication.

I have done a lot of work studying the use of dogs in forensics for criminal investigations. I am working on a study looking at different types of dogs to determine the level of detection capability. I am interested in dogs' ability to identify specific humans. If this capability could be proved scientifically, a dog's "testimony" might perhaps be considered in court. We can train dogs to detect anything that has a distinctive odor. The dog doesn't really care if it's bombs, blood, termites, or crystal meth as long as treats are involved as a reward. Now, no dog will be 100 percent accurate unless given really easy problems, but when you consider the high rate of error in human eyewitness accounts, a dog's ability starts to look pretty good.

CLIFFORD

—— Claudine Singer, Interior designer ——

Clifford was in trouble. As a stray he was involved in a fight and was held at a shelter. He was available only to rescue groups. I volunteered with a local rescue group for fifteen years, so perhaps because Clifford is a golden retriever and I already have Gracie, a golden, I was notified. At the shelter I took him outside to evaluate him, and he just rolled over in the grass. He was obviously a good dog. He seemed to be fine with other dogs. I wish he could tell his story, but I can only surmise that while wandering around as a stray he may have walked up to someone with a dog on a leash. The other dog probably took exception to this, and a fight started. In a situation like this, the stray gets the blame, and Clifford went off to the shelter with a big strike against him.

I never saw any sign of aggression in him and soon found a home for him with a family. They liked him well enough, but he kept figuring out ways to escape from their yard to go wandering. I think he just needed a job. Our rescue group agrees to keep a dog forever, so we will always take one back if things don't work out. I decided to take this one myself.

Like any dog in a new environment, Clifford tried to fit in by marking his terri-tory for days. He was, and still is, an atten-tion-seeking hound; he did a lot of hole digging and nonstop ball fetching, and he found a way to unlatch the pool gate to go swimming. He was a very, very busy boy, and a smart one at that! Whenever he had a chance to bolt out the front door or the garage door, he took it. I frequently chased him down the street. One evening when I was watching TV, I realized that Clifford was very, very slowly and quietly, one foot at a time, climbing up on the couch beside me. Once there, he closed his eyes, thinking perhaps, "She'll never know I'm here." He was kind of irresistible.

In general he fit in nicely. He never had problems with my other dogs or with any dog that came through as a foster. He is quite submissive that way. He's a lover, not a fighter; he rolls over and closes his eyes as if to say, "Don't hurt me, I'm a good boy."

Shortly after Clifford came into our lives, I enrolled him in obedience classes. We started with beginners and moved on to inter-mediate. Then, knowing that I was going to do therapy work with him, I enrolled him in a tricks class. Next I purchased my *Pet Partner's Home Study Manual* from the Delta Society, and we practiced everything he would be tested on. Six months later Clifford graduated at a complex level, ready to begin his career as a therapy dog.

He has turned out to be a real trash-to-treasure dog. For the past four years we have visited various hospitals including a large children's hospital and the Los Angeles Veterans Hospital, nursing homes, and a shelter for battered women and children. Clifford is a Reading Education Assistance Dog, and two years ago he became a HOPE Animal-Assisted Crisis Response Dog. As a HOPE team, our first callout was for a train derailment where ten people died. When we arrived, the victims, both the injured and the dead, had been removed, but we were there to help bring comfort to the rescue workers. We also spent time with families in Mississippi after Hurricane Katrina. During the huge Day Fire in California we visited with fire crews every day for two weeks. It's deeply moving to see these professional people who are under so much stress find comfort by stroking a friendly, sympathetic dog.

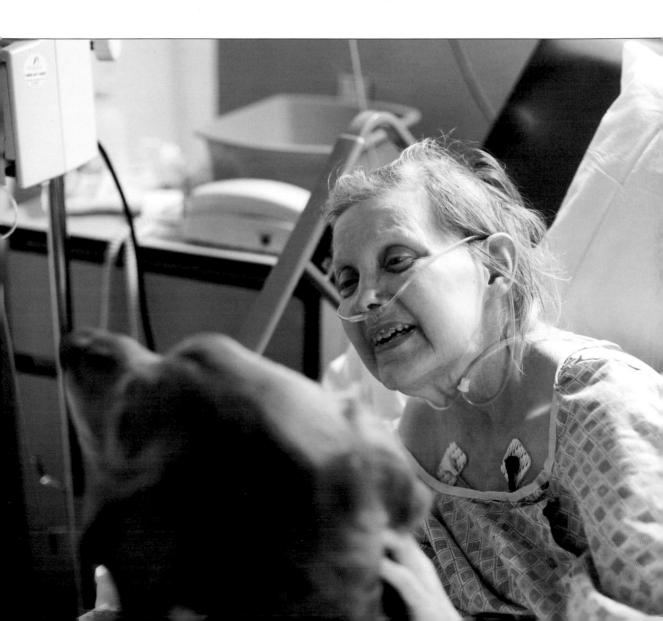

I am working on guidelines for our HOPE work dogs, helping handlers to study their dogs and recognize their stress signals. There are so many variables such as heat, noise levels, modes of travel, and the stress felt by handlers. We train on boats, trains, subways, and planes. It's especially important to know when your dog has had enough, and then know how to help him relax. Clifford is quiet and calm when he's working, but at home all he wants to do is play with his beloved tennis balls. If there's no one around to throw the ball, he will take it to the edge of the pool, drop it in the water, push it forward with his nose, then jump in and retrieve it to start the whole process over again.

Clifford brings all his comfort skills to his hospital visits. Several years ago at the Veterans Hospital a nurse asked me if we could help with a young man who for a week had refused to get out of bed. Clifford walked up to the bed and started butting his head against the side. The man reached down to rub his ears, then he asked Clifford to jump onto the bed, and they started to play. When I suggested taking Clifford for a walk, the young man immediately got up and walked right outside with the dog. The following week the same thing happened. That day Clifford managed to get his new friend interested in throwing the ball for him to retrieve. They did this for half an hour, with everyone happy, including the hospital staff who had despaired of finding an incentive to get their patient out of his depression and out of his bed.

Clifford had a patient once who said that her visit with Clifford made it worth spending three days in the hospital; another said, "I think he knows I'm sad because I just lost my little dog." Recently we were visiting a frail older woman in a hospital bed. She had invited Clifford to get up on the bed, and he was lying quietly beside her in the middle of a jumble of tubes and wires. She was stroking his head; then very slowly and gently he laid his head on her chest. She reached forward quickly, took his ear in her hands and kissed it. It was moving to see, the kind of thing that makes this volunteer work so rewarding. Dogs don't need to be taught about the healing human-animal bond. They know, they already know.

REESE

—— *Danika Marzluff, Student* ——

I adopted Reese when I was nine. I saw her picture on the Northwest Border Collie Rescue Web site. She was eleven months old, huddled up in a ball and looking sad. I was searching for a three-legged dog to adopt because our rescued husky with three legs had died, but when I saw Reese, I knew she was the one for me. My parents helped persuade the rescue group to waive their rule that adopters had to be over twelve.

When Reese was just two months old someone bought her on a whim at a feed store. She went to a home with an Alaskan Malamute, which explains where she learned to howl. She stayed there for about six months, then they called the rescue group. But before a foster home could be found, they gave her to a neighbor. That only lasted a couple of days because their cat terrorized her, and Reese had diarrhea all over the house. She went from there to Sally, who fostered her for three months. Sally had turned down two homes for Reese before we showed up. I guess she liked us. When she brought Reese over to our house the dog seemed to know right away that I was hers. She went straight upstairs to my room, curled up on my bed, and that was

that. Sally had been concerned about our Siberian huskies, but Reese liked them and howled right along with them the first time she heard them.

I always wanted to be involved with pet therapy so I started training Reese. As soon as I was ten (you must be at least ten to be certified with the Delta Society), we passed the certification test to become Pet Partners. My mom became a Partner with Reese too, since an adult needed to accompany us. Mom says that it was much harder for her than it was for me because Reese and I have such a connection.

We visit nursing homes and participate in a Reading With Rover (RWR) program. Last summer we went with the RWR group to a Gilda's Club summer camp for kids from families that are living with cancer. We sat on a blanket in the park while different campers came and read to Reese. She seemed to enjoy it, and the kids did too.

Reese and I have done agility, and she's pretty good at it. We did an agility demo for people at one of the nursing homes we visit. We have even tried herding, which is a natural thing for a border collie. She is very good at learning tricks, and her fans love to watch her.

I'm going into seventh grade in the fall. I'd like to be a veterinarian someday and perhaps work for Veterinarians Without Borders. When I was in Brazil last summer I saw so many desperate, stray dogs. I think there are lots of places where I could help.

ICARUS

—— Gwen Carr, Dog groomer ——

My husband and I adopted Icarus, a Labrador retriever, from our local animal shelter. He was almost four and had been given up to the shelter twice: The first time for unknown reasons, more recently due to a divorce. When we found him, he had been there for two months, attracting little interest. Sometimes people simply don't notice black dogs, and I guess he was too plain and too rambunctious. He badly needed some life skills. I don't think he had been abused in the traditional sense, just neglected, but he did need a job and a sense of purpose, as we all do.

We started out by giving him love, stability, and training. At first we worked on general obedience training, then we moved on to a pet therapy certification course. Once certified, we began visiting an assisted-living facility and a senior center. Icarus has a gentle, friendly nature. He enjoys the residents, and they love him. Some days we visit one on one, at other times we sit in the central hall and people stop to talk to us as they pass by. Many remember his name; some even save crackers or bread for him. They hand me the treats so I can give them to him later. You know how distracting food can be for a dog that really loves it!

Since Icarus was first registered, one of my goals was to visit veterans. A year ago we were cleared to visit the Baltimore Veterans Administration Rehabilitation and Extended Care facility. We were the second therapy dog team approved to visit there. Recently we spent a good deal of time with a Vietnam veteran who can't move his arms or legs. As soon as he sees us, this man starts smiling and calls Icarus over. He likes either me or a staff member to take his hand, place it on Icarus, and move it for him. He always comments on how soft the dog is and sometimes apologizes that he can't move. Beaming, he tells me how much he loves to see Icarus. It makes me happy to see them together. We also visit a young woman who has trouble with movement and speech. She brightens up whenever she sees us coming. Sometimes she can pet a little roughly, but Icarus doesn't mind. You would think that he might get tired of these visits, but he actually seems to look forward to seeing "his" patients. He does all the work, and almost always manages to get people to talk to him, even people who don't like dogs. I'm just the chauffeur.

Even though he is calm around patients, Icarus is still an active, high-energy dog.

He competes in rally obedience and agility. He loves lure coursing, an event where dogs chase a mechanically operated lure that simulates prey such as a jackrabbit or a hare. He's a volunteer blood donor. Staff members at the shelter where we found him wrote an article about Icarus for the local paper to show that older adopted dogs can be successful. Icarus is certainly living proof of that!

JENNA

—— *Janell Keider, Part-time dog trainer, full-time mom* ——

I had just been told that I would not live to see my kids grow up, and I knew that I had to have one more dog in my life. My husband and I set out to search for my last dog. I wanted a puppy, a short-haired puppy, because our daughter had asthma, but at the

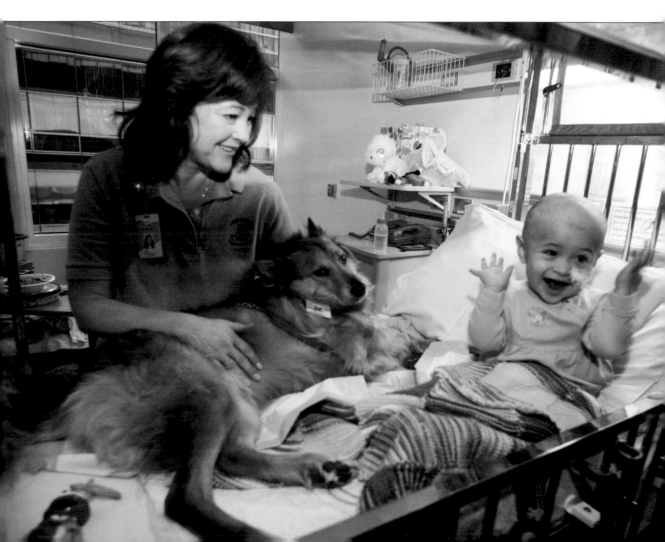

third and last shelter of the day, my husband suggested that we walk through the adult section. At the back of a pen, I spotted a little ball of fur, about four months old, definitely long-haired. She ran forward and jumped up with her little front paws on the cage door. My husband and I were hooked on the spot. We took her home as soon as she had been spayed.

The next week, Jenna came down with a very serious case of parvovirus and nearly died. Whenever I came to visit her at the veterinary hospital, she tried to wag her tail. I knew she was fighting hard to survive. There was something very special about her. When she was well enough to come home, we both slept in the laundry room, and I fed her small bits of soft food every few hours. She made it.

And I made it too. We learned that my original diagnosis was totally wrong. Jenna is now six years old. We have been a pet therapy team for three years, and I often share her story with patients at Children's Hospital of Orange County. It helps the kids to know that Jenna was very sick and in the hospital but now is well and so happy to be visiting them. We average two to three visits each month, and spend two or three hours on the inpatient, outpatient, rehab, and clinic floors. Jenna is also trained in agility and she puts this to use in rehab as she encourages children to follow her through tunnels, up and down steps, even down a slide. In the ortho clinic, I feel so proud of her as she sits next to a child on a gurney while a cast-removal saw whirs over her head and the frightened child cries and hangs on to her fur. Jenna doesn't seem to mind the strong smell of chemo treatments; she will lie next to children in the cancer clinic before and after their treatments. She is especially good at snuggling and warming their little bodies. We are there for the staff and for the families too.

One day we passed a waiting room at the hospital, and a mom motioned me to come in. Her daughter was there, about seven years old, in a wheelchair. She was a double amputee at the knee level, without prostheses. The little girl was excited to meet Jenna. After she had seen Jenna's tricks and petted her for a while, the child asked if she could take Jenna for a walk. I glanced at her mom who nodded, so I said O.K. The child slid off her wheelchair and reached for the end of the leash while I held the middle. Balancing on protectors on the ends of her legs, she said, "Jenna, heel," and off we went. Jenna stayed right next to the child, carefully "heeling" so there was no tension on the leash. The little girl beamed from ear to ear as she worked to walk down the hallway, past the patient rooms, and back to the waiting room. When she stumbled once, Jenna froze and leaned closer as the child put her hand on the dog's back to catch her balance. Then we continued. Some people were staring, but the little girl just kept on smiling and telling everyone, "I'm walking the dog!" I don't think I have ever been prouder of my beloved Jenna.

SUNNY

—— *Valarie Franklin, Pharmacy student* ——

Sunny is my service dog. It was Natalie Sachs-Ericsson who rescued him so she should tell that part of his story.

Natalie: A friend of mine, Diane Maxfield, was driving down one of the busiest streets in town when she spotted a golden retriever on the median. She stopped her car right in the middle of traffic and persuaded the dog to get in. Sunny was in pretty rough shape, a flea-ridden intact male with heartworm. Diane had him cleaned up, neutered, and treated for heartworm. He had a sweet temperament so she called me. Years ago I started the Leon County Service-to-Shelter Dog Program. I rescue potential service dogs from shelters and give them basic training and socializing before turning them over to service dog training organizations.

Because Diane has her own rescued golden retriever, a dog that has made a huge difference with her autistic child, she wanted Sunny to go to a program where he could help a child. I have been working primarily for Paws With a Cause. At that time they almost never had children among their clients. When I explained this to Diane, she agreed to donate Sunny anyway because she thought he could help someone. Several months later, Valarie, a sophomore in high school, applied to Paws for a dog. She was initially told that it might take up to three years to get one suitable for her but in only a few months she got a call from Paws to tell her about Sunny.

In the meantime, Sunny had performed well on a temperament test that typically has a 50 percent failure rate. I worked with him for the following three months, and he was great. Then one day we were training in a busy mall and a pneumatic drill went off right beside us just as the nearby merry-go-round started twirling with lights and horns blaring. Sunny panicked and nearly took my arm off trying to bolt. I almost washed him from the program but Lynn Hoekstra, the Paws head trainer, asked me to try to work it out. Well, there happened to be a Wendy's near the merry-go-round so before each training session, I bought twenty cheeseburgers and stuffed them in my backpack. At first we hung out sixty feet away from the merry-go-round, and Sunny ate cheeseburgers. I fed Sunny cheeseburgers for many days—hours of cheeseburgers as we very slowly worked our way closer and closer. It was a lot of work but after two weeks, we were riding on the merry-go-round together—more cheeseburgers!

I was delighted but still a little unsure: What if some strange new noise went off, and the dog bolted? He could seriously hurt his client. I took him to the other mall in town in search of a novel and noisy place to try out my concerns, but I couldn't find anything challenging. Then I noticed a police car parked near a coffee shop. I went in and asked the police officer if he was planning to go to his car any time soon. He looked at me (and at the dog), raised his eyebrows and said, "Should I be going to the car soon?" When I explained my problem, he said, "Sure, I'll help you."

We went outside and the officer got in his car while Sunny and I approached slowly. Just as we reached the car the policeman turned on his siren and the flashing lights started to twirl. Sunny sat down, looked up at me (I swear he was grinning) and in his eyes I could read what he was thinking: "Where is my cheeseburger?" We flew up to Michigan the next day for his advanced training. Paws trainers worked with Sunny and then decided that he and Valarie would be a good team.

Valarie: When I went to the Paws headquarters in Wayland, Michigan, to meet Sunny, I was sixteen and a sophomore in high school. I had never had a dog before Sunny, and I was very nervous. I was afraid he wouldn't like me. When the trainer brought the dog out, Sunny came right up to me and sniffed my face, wagging his tail. We started training together immediately. He opened doors for me and picked things up off the floor. It was a little hard to get him to work for me because he kept looking at the trainer when I gave him commands, and sometimes instead of bringing things to me, he took them to her. Still I knew he was amazing. I have a brittle bone disease, and Paws selected Sunny for me because of his

gentle nature. My mom had always told me that some day I would get a special dog, but even after we applied, I had expected to wait for years until they found the right dog. As it turned out, I only waited about six months because Sunny showed up (thank you, Natalie, thank you, Diane!).

I went home, and Sunny stayed to continue his training. Three months later, during spring break I returned to Wayland for some more work together, but this time I was going to take the dog home with me. I remember being worried that he wouldn't listen to me; his focus still seemed to be on the trainer. Before we left I went into the bathroom and took him with me. When we were alone, he listened to me. He lay down when I told him to, and came to me when I called his name. This experience broke my fear because I realized that once it was just the two of us, he would respond to me.

Still, it was quite an adjustment for both of us. I had to do everything for Sunny so that he would focus on me. At first my parents were not supposed to feed him or even touch him. I was used to going out with my friends, but now if I went somewhere without Sunny, he would have to stay home in a room by himself. He was a comfort and a help, but also a responsibility. I had a lot to learn. Sunny knew his tasks, but I had to be a better trainer. I had to give him commands in a tone of voice that would make him pay attention. My field instructors, Lori Grigg and Mark Bills, would say, "*Tell* him to do it, don't *ask* him!" Fortunately I had lots of help. Lori and Mark were great. They came to my house frequently, and we often took Sunny to places where we could practice commands in the real world. We learned to work as a team. By the end of my sopho-more year, Sunny was coming to school with me at least three days a week. In the fall we became certified. I took ownership of Sunny and we were entitled to all the benefits of service dog certification. Lori and Mark have helped me so much. A service dog is an ongoing project, so I still work with Lori, although she is no longer affiliated with Paws. She has a program called For Better Independence Assistance Dogs. My parents have helped me a lot too. Sunny stays with them if I have to go somewhere without him. They love him, and my dad spoils him a little more than he should!

Sunny does many things for me. He can get help if I need it; he will find someone in the house and lead them back to me. He can push an emergency button, bring me the phone, and retrieve items I drop. He pushes automatic door buttons and pulls regular doors open for me. I have developed a problem in my knee that makes climbing up and down stairs painful and sometimes impossible. Sunny lets me lean on him going down, and he walks one step ahead of me on the way up to give me a little momentum.

He is well-trained of course, but I think he is also just naturally a good dog. He loves me and is concerned about me. He watches me and follows me, sometimes looking a little worried, his eyebrows moving around while he takes everything in. When he's asleep, and I try to be extra quiet as I go to the next room to grab a book or something, he always wakes up as soon as I move. I live by myself now in my own apartment near college, and Sunny is good company.

Sunny makes life easier for me in a physical sense, but his greatest contribution is in changing the way other people look at me. My disability is very obvious: I am only three feet tall. When I go places alone, people stare, little kids point, and it can be very hurtful. When Sunny is with me, everyone looks at him and admires him. Sunny is cute and adorable and way more interesting than I am. Kids point at the pretty dog and don't even notice me. And that's just fine!

Sunny is almost nine now; we've been together for seven years—seven great years.

JITTERBUG

—— *Maryanne Dell, Journalist* ——

Because of my rescue work, I receive a lot of e-mails about dogs and cats that need help. I take in animals from time to time and find homes for them. One day an e-mail arrived describing a small dog available only to rescue groups because she was severely injured and couldn't use her hind legs. Something about her picture reminded me of an old dog of mine so I went to look at her, expecting to take her and place her if she was a nice dog. Well, at the shelter this little thing dragged herself right over to me. Her back feet were bloody but she was wagging her tail. What could I do?

I've never been a small-dog person, which is one reason I didn't figure I would keep Jitterbug, a Tibetan spaniel, but after two days in my house, this dog took up residence in my heart. She was listed as a stray, had scars that could have been puncture wounds, and of course the paralysis, but I still can't imagine that no one came looking for her. She has the greatest personality: She's always happy, her little tail goes constantly, and she has the cutest snaggle-toothed grin. Tibbies are bred to have underbites, and hers is pretty darn severe.

I took her to a neurologist to check out her back. The diagnosis was a herniated disc, paralyzing both hind legs. The neurologist said surgery *might* restore function but it would cost $4400. I collected enough donations to pay about half the costs, but I probably would have done it anyway—after all, what are credit cards for?

The surgery was successful, and now Jitterbug walks, hops, trots, and runs just fine. She's so mellow and sociable I knew right away that I wanted her to become a Delta Society Pet Partner. We worked on training (I'm an evaluator for Delta so I knew the drill), and less than a year after I had adopted her we got our complex rating. We visit a skilled nursing facility, an assisted-living facility, plus inpatients, and an outpatient therapy group at a local hospital.

Jitterbug is also a Reading Education Assistance Dog at a school where we work with students whose reading skills need improvement. One of our first students, a little girl who was painfully shy, barely spoke at first. When she tried to read a simple book, she could hardly get the words out. I asked her to explain some of the pictures to Jitterbug, and that got her talking a little, but as soon as the session ended she left with a quick whispered, "Goodbye."

At our next session I asked her about her cats and then told her Jitterbug's story—her injury, the successful surgery, how I fell in love with her and decided to keep her. That seemed to open the floodgates, and this shy child started jabbering, petting Jitter, talking about her family and her pets, and, best of all, trying hard to read. By the end of the school year, her reading had improved more than any of our other students, and it was all Jitterbug's doing. If she hadn't been there, I could have talked until I ran out of breath, and it wouldn't have made any difference to this timid child. It was the little dog, quiet and unassuming, that did it all.

I love the light in people's eyes when they see her. At the therapy group we met a woman who was totally closed, not meeting anyone's eyes, not speaking. But when I brought Jitterbug over to her, she smiled. Nowadays she eagerly asks to hold her and she talks to us both. Recently, we sat on the couch next to a woman I hadn't seen before. She started petting Jitter and talking, telling me about her mother's death and then losing her mother's dog soon after. She talked for about ten minutes, stroking Jitterbug the whole time. Then she thanked me, saying it felt good to share this story she hadn't felt able to tell anyone before.

I just can't believe how lucky I am to have stumbled across this little dog and to be sharing my life with her. If I had not opened that e-mail, she might not be here, and the people she helps might not get the benefits she brings them. It's almost heart-stopping.

LUCY

—— *Dorothy Diehl, Marriage and family therapist* ——

In 2002 I had surgery to remove a benign tumor on one side of my face. The surgeon severed the main facial nerve and damaged the auditory nerve. I became completely deaf in that ear, my balance was affected, and one side of my face was totally paralyzed. I would need a number of surgeries to try to correct some of the

problems caused by the paralysis. I was forty-nine, single, and had always enjoyed a very active life. I became self-conscious about my face and my deafness and struggled with depression resulting from the consequences of the surgery.

My animals were a real comfort. At that time I had two cats and some rabbits. Before the surgery, I had started a nonprofit domestic rabbit rescue, Bunnies Urgently Needing Shelter (BUNS). I had always hoped to own a dog eventually. Then one day when a friend and I were talking about assistance dogs, I realized that I could get a hearing dog. I looked on the Internet and discovered the San Francisco SPCA Hearing Dog program. I was especially pleased that this hearing dog would come from a shelter. I learned that I was eligible for a dog even though my deafness is single-sided. I sleep on my good ear so I can't hear the alarm clock or the smoke detector. With deafness in one ear, I lost the sense of the direction of sounds. Sometimes when friends came to my house, I had no idea they were there.

I filled out a four-page application, and a month or two later learned that I had been accepted for the waiting list. Over the course of a year, three or four classes graduated, each with six or seven dogs. After every graduation I called to see where I was on the list.

In the meantime someone from the SPCA had discovered Lucy at a rural shelter where the adoption rate was low and the euthanasia rate, high. The dog's hair was long and matted, and she was covered with ticks and fleas, but she definitely had personality. Since she seemed adoptable she went to the SPCA for their regular adoption program, but after a few days Glenn Martyn spotted her for the hearing dog program. Lucy is very smart; she learned basic obedience quickly. She is highly motivated by rewards

of treats and praise. She soon started sound work and learned to alert to a doorbell, a telephone ring, an alarm clock, and a smoke detector. She was a bit fearful and absolutely terrified at the thought of getting into a car, but Glenn helped her through that issue pretty creatively. He parked his van with the open door right against the door to the house. Excited to go out (maybe a walk!), Lucy raced through the door and found herself in the car with lots of praise and delicious treats. Glenn repeated variations on this exercise until she lost her fear of cars.

Since Lucy had a lot of energy, plus some residual fears, Glenn wanted to place her with someone who was both active and gentle. He thought we could work well together. He knew that I had cats and rabbits so he took Lucy to a pet shop with rabbits and she completely ignored them. She wasn't too sure about cats, but he felt she could learn to live with mine. Glenn really believed in Lucy even though she had some issues. In April 2004 he came to interview me, to check me out and to take a look at my house and yard with Lucy in mind. He decided that we were a good match.

Eventually I went to San Francisco to meet Lucy and train with her at the San Francisco Hearing Dog Program. When I first saw the dog, I wasn't so sure. She had this horrible haircut—a furry face attached to a skinny, shaved body. She was very wiggly and kept jumping up in the air. I took a deep breath and thought, "Well, let's just see where this goes."

The week went well. It was great to work with Glenn. We practiced basic obedience: sit, stay, down. We did sound work, encouraging Lucy to nudge me as an alert to the doorbell, the alarm clock, and the smoke alarm. Everything went well; Lucy could do all the stuff. I felt very privileged to have that week in San Francisco where I learned how the training actually works. Sadly, the hearing dog program has been closed down, but Glenn has joined the faculty at the Assistance Dog Institute at the Bergin University of Canine Studies.

I was very happy to finally take Lucy home with me. She tried hard and was awfully good, and in six months she was settled in. I used to attach her leash to my belt and go out to do bunny chores. This worked well, and gradually she became more accustomed to my life in general. Now Lucy and the cats all sleep on the bed together. I think cats actually like to have a dog around for protection: If Lucy is out in the yard, they often choose to go out too.

It was always obvious that Lucy enjoyed the training exercises. She was so smart and happy to please that I wanted to keep on training her. In the process of searching for an advanced obedience class, I met a trainer who recommended (and taught) agility. Lucy caught on right away. She loved the physical challenge, the running and jumping, and she loved getting out and being around other dogs and people. Lucy aced the beginner classes and breezed through the next two levels. She now has many agility titles. Among other awards, she recently won the highest title awarded by the U.S. Dog Agility Association at the performance level.

Working with Lucy in training and competition has changed my life. The thing about agility is that people aren't looking at your face. Agility competition is centered on the dog/handler team, but spectators tend to watch the dog. The whole process was good for me both physically and mentally. I had to concentrate, to watch Lucy, to think and run. The handler must memorize the course, sometimes a challenging exercise. Early in our career, as Lucy came out of the tunnel at one event, I was a little disoriented and unsure, but with no guide from me, Lucy went straight to a jump—and it was the right one. I realized then that she had been paying attention the whole time. Working together has brought us very close. We have a good intuitive connection. Sometimes when I'm saying one thing but thinking another, Lucy will do what I'm thinking. Dogs pick up on all your cues.

Lucy is predominantly golden retriever with a marvelous face. Her picture used to be on the donation envelope for the San Francisco SPCA so you can just imagine how appealing she is. An adorable Golden Girl. She has a good life. She comes to work with me where she sleeps in the reception area and greets my clients. As a therapist, I see people who have been discarded by their families, but when someone takes an interest and believes in them, it can make all the difference. Glenn Martyn gave Lucy that kind of chance.

And Lucy has saved my life. When she came to me, I was feeling bad. I was self-conscious, lost, depressed. Just going out to walk around the block was hard, but Lucy loved going out so we went. We started visiting the off-leash park and began agility, first the training classes, then competition. All this expanded my world. Once, driving home from a show, I looked over at Lucy, lying there asleep, and I thought about the way her life had changed. She was a stray wandering the streets, now she's a champion. And I went from that awful post-surgery despair to a whole different life. We have done so much for each other.

HUEY, APOLLO, CHANDLER, and JOEY

—— Elizabeth Rivard, Director, Prison Pet Partnership ——

—— Rachel Malay, Connie Mawyer, Mary Kniskern, and Cassie Scott, Inmates ——

Elizabeth Rivard: The mission for the Prison Pet Partnership at the Washington Corrections Center for Women is to rescue and train homeless dogs to be service dogs for people with disabilities. We also operate a boarding kennel and grooming facility to provide vocational education for women inmates. Inmates train the dogs and run the boarding kennel and grooming facility, and they gain clerical skills working in our office. Revenues from boarding and grooming supply about half our program budget, and six percent of that budget is covered by prison funds for vocational education. We raise the rest through private donations and grants.

In order to qualify for the program, inmates must have no major infractions for a year and no minor infractions for ninety days. No one with a history of abuse toward children or animals may apply. Once accepted, the inmate employee must pass a three-month pet care technician class that covers grooming, kennel care, first aid, pet health and wellness maintenance, and customer-relations skills. Once she passes the course, she is assigned a dog, sometimes two dogs.

We have a waiting list for service dogs and a waiting list of inmates applying for the program. We currently have fourteen women in the program here, and we hope to expand to the two minimum security women's facilities in the state in an effort to provide ongoing opportunities for women from our facility as they transition back into the community. Over the years, of the 140 program participants for whom we have records, only four have reoffended, a rate of 3 percent, compared to a state recidivism rate for women of 35 percent.

Only one in every fifteen or twenty dogs actually becomes a service dog. The others are adopted as paroled pets. They have had good training so there's a waiting list for them too. If we bred our own dogs for the program we would probably have a higher success rate, but our mission is to provide a second chance—for the inmates, for the disabled people who benefit from the dogs, and for the animals themselves.

Connie: I have two dogs, and it's full-time work. My dogs spend twenty-four hours a day with me. Huey, a Labrador/Swiss mountain dog mix, is young enough, good enough, and versatile enough to become almost any kind of service dog. He's very loving, and he likes to work. Working is for Huey like play is for most dogs. His size makes him a good possibility for mobility and support assistance. I will focus on harness work and wheelchair work for him. When we have a potential person in mind for him, I can tailor the training to whatever is needed.

This is probably the first place in their lives where these dogs have a normal routine with regular food, exercise, and leadership. Many of them have been neglected in backyards or were running loose with other dogs. With a new dog I spend the first few months building a strong bond, the most important route to a successful service dog. I give the dog food, toys, and attention. I try to be

creative and make his day exciting; he learns to keep his eye on me. Most of the dogs are under two years old when we start training, and many are just puppies in big dog bodies. I try to be sympathetic and remember that I had some growing up and maturing to do. What I learn from this dog will help with my next dog. It's emotional work and exciting. Every day we can see every dog improve. We can see that what we do makes a difference. This improves confidence and self-esteem for us and for the dogs.

There is a kind of magic in seeing the difference a dog can make in the life of a disabled person. After all, people who need these dogs are in a different kind of prison. They each have their own needs. They want to be able to leave their homes or get around better or let a spouse go to work. Over time, the owners' needs may change and increase, but since dogs are pack animals, I believe that they have the ability to adjust to the person who has become a member of their pack, in a sense.

Mary: I'm working with Chandler, the long-legged golden retriever. He spent six months with Rachel, and now he's with me. We're trying to build his confidence with different people. He's learning that he's safe. It's so important to condition the dogs not to be afraid of things, to be confident. Chandler is learning that he doesn't have to make all the decisions. He can let me make most of them, and I think that will be a great relief for him.

Cassie: I've been training dogs for three years. It's a twenty-four-hour job but I love it. One of my dogs now works with a woman in a wheelchair. Apollo, a husky/shar-pei mix, is my fifth dog. He likes to greet people. He loves kids, he loves everybody. He'll probably work at a nursing home. He goes out now once a week to visit seniors, and I know he makes them happy.

Rachel: I work with Joey, the Labrador, teaching him about wheelchairs and how to walk beside someone for support. He's also learning how to open and close doors: regular doors, doors with push buttons, and cabinet doors. Eventually he's going to make a big difference in someone's life. Will I be sad when he goes? I'll miss him, of course, but I see how excited he is when a volunteer comes to take him out in the world even for an afternoon. So I'll be happy when he gets to go outside of here and live in a home.

LINUS

—— Melissa Torbik, Hospital pharmaceutical representative ——

—— Chris de Villeneuve, Managing director, real estate firm ——

Melissa: When he was just seven weeks old I adopted Linus at my local Petco, which hosts shelter adoption days every week. He's a hound (maybe beagle) and shepherd mix. Linus came to me with four perfect legs, but when he was seven months old he was hit by a taxi and lost a leg. He quickly adapted to life on three legs, and his cheerful attitude never changed. He remained as sweet as ever.

Chris: I met Linus when I began dating his mother/owner, Melissa. I fell in love with this dog immediately as most people do. He was two years old, not only beautiful but also intelligent, intuitive, and lots of fun. He seemed to trust and like everyone; he felt at ease sidling up to any stranger sitting on a stoop, often rolling over for a belly rub. He was perfectly comfortable with his city lifestyle, never spooked by car noise, yelling, bicycles, or joggers. He walked around the neighborhood as if he was the mayor campaigning for reelection, confident and personable. He knew exactly where to get dog treats—at the florist, the antique shop, and the video store. He knew where to find "people" food, such as a piece of pepperoni at the pizza joint or a bit of grilled chicken at the Middle Eastern place. His friendliness was an inspiration to me. I felt that the world would be a better place if more people knew Linus.

One day I read an article about therapy dogs and what it took to be a good one. I knew right away that Linus fit every requirement and then some. He was a natural. Soon I discovered that the Delta Society was holding pet therapy certification classes within walking distance of our apartment, and the rest is history! Linus passed the tests, one with Melissa, one with me. We all became certified.

Linus is one of the founding therapy dogs in the Paws for Patients program at New York Presbyterian Hospital/Weill Cornell Medical Center. Every Tuesday afternoon he and I visit the inpatient rehabilitation unit. As soon as I put on his work vest and his ID badge, he runs over to stand by the door, ready to go. At the hospital we find a group of patients assembled in the activity room waiting for Linus. He runs down the hall to greet them, shaking hands all around and performing a few other tricks. Then the patients work on their rehabilitation goals: Some throw the ball for him to fetch, some practice balance and coordination while walking with him, then some people groom him using their fine and gross motor skills. He distracts people and makes the exercises fun. Most of our patients are amazed that the dog gets around so well with only three legs. Some comment that he doesn't seem to even notice that he has a disability. He encourages people every day. I have heard patients say, "If he can do it, I can too!"

After the group work, we visit some patients in their rooms. Sad, scared, even grouchy people brighten up for Linus. I think his disability creates a bond with these people who are struggling with physical challenges of their own.

Melissa: Linus recently won the Plane Tree Award for nontraditional therapy with hospital patients. He and his work have been featured on two local news channels and in the *New York Daily News*. He brings love and joy to every life he touches. He seems to recognize people who need him: Sometimes he goes up to total strangers and sits with them. Often people say, "Thanks, I really needed that today."

We used to visit a florist shop where one of the men always gave Linus biscuits. The guy left for another job, so for months we didn't stop there. One day Linus really wanted to go in, so we did. Some of the guys remembered him and found some dog treats for him. After a short visit, we left. As we were walking down the street, a man we hadn't seen in the shop came running after us, yelling to me. When he caught up, he asked if Linus worked at Cornell Medical in the rehab department. I said yes. He then proceeded to tell me that he had broken his back a couple of years before and had been stuck in the hospital rehabilitation center recuperating for a long, long time. He'd been frustrated and miserable. It sometimes seemed that he would never get out and be himself again. But there was a bright part in every week: a visit with Linus. He told me that he always looked forward to seeing Linus; those visits got him through a long, dreary time.

Linus specializes in brightening people's days. Whenever Chris and I see those smiles lighting up faces that were anxious and tense, we know that it's no exaggeration to call him a miracle dog.

GINA

—— Pam Bertz, Attorney ——

From what we have been able to learn about her (don't you wish dogs could talk?), it seems that Gina spent the first eight months of her life with a kind woman who loved and pampered her. Then, when an emergency arose, this woman could no longer keep her. The dog went to a family with an angry and abusive father who often threw things and hit his wife and kids. For almost a year Gina suffered along with the rest of the family, until one day the man took her into the desert and dumped her there. She wandered around until she was picked up and taken to a shelter where she stayed for two months. She eventually ended up on the kill list just before we found her on a Web site and adopted her.

At first she was very skinny with stomach problems. Her coat was hard, ragged, and wiry from malnutrition. She certainly didn't look anything like a golden retriever, but we decided to take her anyway. She was about eighteen months old. We already had Cinder, another rescued golden, and Gina was happy to play with her. She thrived on good food and care. Her beautiful golden retriever coat came in. Life was looking pretty good for Gina, but there was a man in the house (my husband), and

at first she avoided him at all costs. She was terrified of all men and boys.

But this man was different. He talked softly, didn't try to hit or kick, gave good things for breakfast, and treats at night. Best of all, Cinder didn't seem afraid of him. Slowly, Gina began to approach my husband and ask to be petted. He stroked her gently and talked softly to her. Could it be that not all men were bad?

Cinder was already certified for animal-assisted therapy work, and she loved it, bouncing around with excitement whenever I brought out her vest before a visit. Gina seemed interested so I started training her, explaining that she would have to be nice to everyone, including men. About a year after we adopted her, she passed her certification test with flying colors. Her first visit was at an adult daycare center with lots of men. She stopped for a minute at the door and looked up at me. Then she marched right over to those men and wagged her tail.

Gina put all her fears and bad memories behind her. For the past five years she has visited assisted living homes, the Casa Youth Shelter, and patients at Hoag Hospital. As a HOPE Animal-Assisted Crisis Response dog, she and Cinder spend time

with first responders at fire camps and with people displaced by fires who are staying in shelters.

Gina's greatest accomplishment took place at the youth shelter, where she changed the life of a young man we'll call J. As we introduced ourselves to the group, I told them that when she was young, Gina had been abused by a man to the point where she avoided all men and boys because she was afraid they might hit or kick her. I noticed a boy about sixteen years old in the back row, looking interested. We then went to the recreation room for one-on-one work with the kids. J immediately claimed Gina; she jumped up on the couch beside him and laid her head on his lap. He petted her and talked to her for about forty-five minutes. We took pictures of the kids with the dogs. J wanted only Gina in his picture. He hung this picture in his room and labeled it "my girlfriend."

Later I learned that since his arrival at the shelter J had tried to stay in the background as much as he could. Gina missed our next scheduled visit because I was sick. J was disappointed, ignored the other dogs, and stayed by himself. On the following visit, Gina trotted in and looked around for her friend. J had stayed in his room, but as soon as he heard that Gina was there, he hurried out and joined the group in the recreation room. When Gina saw him come in, she ran to him and laid her head in his lap. For about forty-five minutes J talked to Gina, and she listened, content and happy. When we moved downstairs for pictures she followed him.

After the next few visits J seemed to have a breakthrough. He began to talk to others more freely, and did better in school. He wanted to know how Gina could put the abuse behind her, have forgiveness in her heart, and now seem to love everyone. As we talked about these questions, J gained more confidence, and I think he began to realize that he too could try to put his abusive past behind him. He wanted to learn the obedience signals and commands so I helped him work with Gina, and with him she was a model student. Through his work with Gina, J's self-esteem rose, he got a part-time job and, with an improved GPA, he became a drum major in his high school band. Eventually he found a nice permanent home, just like Gina did. He graduated high school, and I hear he got a puppy of his own to train and was thinking of becoming a Pet Partner.

Gina still looks for J every time we visit the youth shelter, but I think she knows that he has a better life now, and that she helped make it happen. She made that rare connection with J, a young man who was struggling with an abusive past similar to hers. The bond benefited them both.

Gina has continued her work at the shelter: She teaches the kids about compassion and, in return, gets lots of hugs, kisses, and stories.

SADIE, the ARSON DOG

—— *Fred Andes, Fire captain, Phoenix Fire Department* ——

Sadie, a chocolate Labrador, was abandoned when she was pretty young. Her owners moved away and left her behind, tied to the barn door. She seemed to have potential as a working dog and ended up being trained for arson detection work. Labs and Lab mixes are often used for arson detection. They tend to have good noses and are friendly and enthusiastic about working for treats.

State Farm Insurance has provided over 200 arson dogs across the United States and in Canada. They paid more than $20,000 to train Sadie and then to train me to work with her. She's pretty valuable for an abandoned dog. Sadie's job is to let

me know if an accelerant like lighter fluid or gasoline was used to start a fire. This information helps determine where and how the fire started. She is trained to sit when she detects an accelerant, whether it is on a piece of charred wood or carpet or on the shoes or hands of an arson suspect. Without Sadie's help, gathering evidence can be a hit-or-miss deal. She cuts down on the guesswork. Not all fires are caused by accelerants but if they are, a trained dog can help the investigation, saving time and resources. When investigations go more quickly, thousands of taxpayer dollars are saved. Property owners and insurance companies benefit when claims can be cleared more quickly.

I take Sadie everywhere with me. We go to fire scenes, of course, and she hangs out with me at the office or in my truck or at home. To keep her sharp we have an ongoing training program. Sadie doesn't have a regular meal schedule. She gets small snacks throughout the day, and she earns them. Each morning I measure out Sadie's rations for the day and then dole it out as rewards in practice searches and when she's working. I put gasoline or lighter fluid on pieces of charred carpet or clothes and store them in cans. Then I hide the cans at the fire station, in my house, or other places. Every once in a while in the course of our day I tell her to search, and when she identifies the right can, she gets a handful of dog food.

Sadie and I conduct our arson detection work in many different situations. Recently we were called to the site of a vehicle fire. Three handcuffed suspects were sitting on the curb. I walked Sadie around them to search for a scent of the gas found on the partially burned car seat. She sniffed the men's shoes, their pants, and their hands. Then she stopped in front of one guy and sat down. He was questioned and later confessed to setting the fire. You can't lie to a dog when she sits down in front of you because she can smell gasoline on your hands.

FRED

—— Diane Shust, Attorney ——

My daughter and I were walking our dog, Wags, in the park when we first saw Fred. He was painfully thin and ragged, with large patches of exposed skin. I said to my daughter, "We'd better get out of here quick!" I knew he was a stray, and I knew we would want to keep him. I was a single mom. I already had my hands full with one child, one dog, and one cat.

We watched the dog wander into the basketball court. Then a boy kicked him when he got in the way. I raced over, the boy apologized for kicking my dog, but by then Fred was running away. I chased him

down a hill with train tracks at the bottom and somehow managed to lure him to me. I picked him up (he weighed less than twenty pounds) and carried him home while my nine-year-old daughter walked beside us with Wags on the leash. I called the Humane Society and then immediately fell in love with the scruffy little dog.

I had adopted Wags from a shelter, and I contributed to the Humane Society so I knew that I had to call them in case someone had reported this dog as missing. I'm a lawyer and a do-gooder, and I tend to do the right thing, but by the time the Humane Society officer arrived, my daughter and I were both crying and sobbing. He took Fred away, but he told us that when the shelter opened at 7:30 the next morning, we could put our names on the list to adopt the dog. Well, we were there at 7:25. No one claimed him during the holding period, and the rest is history.

We were so fortunate to get Fred. He's extremely good natured and sweet. Perhaps due to his previous life of neglect and starvation, he'll eat anything. This is not always a healthy trait. Once he chewed the top off a container of Motrin and swallowed all the pills. He was seriously sick with kidney failure so now he's on a very low-protein diet, and this may have inspired him: He started opening the refrigerator. The first time, I thought I hadn't closed it properly; the second and third times I thought the rubber gasket on the door was worn out.

He likes midnight snacks; once he dropped a baked potato on my pillow at 4 AM. He and Wags woke me one night growling over a bag of salad mix, each tugging on an end of the bag. Fred likes fruit salad, pasta, any kind of leftovers, but especially protein. One day I noticed a funny smell in the living room and discovered part of a roast chicken he had hidden behind the sofa cushions. Try explaining that to the dry cleaner! Now the refrigerator is secured with a bungee cord.

About six years ago I read about the Humane Society's humane education program. I talked to the program manager and volunteered with Fred. He passed a temperament test with flying colors, and for the past six years we have been visiting students at Ross School. When we're a block or two from the school, Fred sits up and starts wagging his tail. He walks around the classroom, visits with everyone, and gets loved. We talk about caring for animals, and the kids write stories about Fred and draw pictures of him. Once, a little boy who was terrified of dogs stayed in the back of the room, as far away from Fred as possible. But little by little, week by week, Fred gained his confidence until one day the child came right up to him. When another dog came to visit, the boy said, "Well, I guess I will pat him if he's a friend of Fred's."

Fred knows exactly where his classroom is. Sometimes he refuses to leave. He just lies on the rug and looks at me. He loves being with the kids.

SCOTCH

*—— Diane McGuire, Administrative assistant,
city development services department ——*

At three, Scotch was a throwaway dog left to fend for himself on the mean streets of Phoenix. The first time I saw this dog—part border collie, part Australian shepherd, part neighborhood Romeo—he was leading a motley cast of neighborhood dogs and assorted strays on that morning's adventure.

He was a striking, large, black-and-white dog with a plumed tail waving happily. He had one eye marked like a bandit, giving his face a rakish, devil-may-care expression. He bounded along, inviting his followers to a game of doggie tag. The pack romped and played for most of the morning. After that

day I saw the big dog often around the neighborhood with his favorite companion, a cute little pug, trotting alongside. Midmorning he could be found enjoying the sun, curled up on a pile of dried horse manure at a nearby horse ranch.

This vagabond life came to an abrupt end one day. I found Scotch on the edge of a busy road, his eyes fixed on his little friend the pug lying still in the middle of the road while the morning commuter traffic whizzed by her. The big dog lay there anxiously watching his friend, his heart in his eyes. Although it was too late to save the pug, I stopped traffic long enough to remove her from the road. I was so touched by Scotch's loyalty and devotion that I decided to take him home with me. Once there, he was welcomed with varying levels of enthusiasm by the others who share my home: Queenie and Huck, the Cardigan corgis; Scooter, a papillon; Mac, an Ibizan hound; Bailey, a yellow Labrador; Auggie, a Doberman cross; Buster, a border collie; Tonto, a pit bull cross with perhaps a bit of greyhound; Xena and Mr. Ziggy, the miniature dachshunds; Kenny, a twenty-pound cat; and last, but certainly not least, Patrick, my mealy Amazon parrot and Skeeter, a Myers parrot. Queenie, Scooter, Mac, and Kenny the cat are all Delta Society registered therapy animals.

In time Scotch adjusted to life in my house. We started obedience classes. He proved to be a quick study, well-behaved, mellow, and kind. He soon passed the Delta Society therapy dog exam. Over the years, we have visited a variety of facilities working with different populations. At a health-care facility we would often find patients waiting for Scotch at the door on our visiting day. He is savvy around wheelchairs, oxygen tanks, and other paraphernalia. He greets everyone happily, always gently adjusting his behavior with stroke victims and people who have lost the use of limbs. In one ward with "difficult" patients, many residents would light up when they saw this big dog coming toward them with his tail wagging. One man who had been curled up on the floor the first time we saw him, got right up on another visit and gave Scotch a big hug. I had never heard the man speak before, but that day he said, "I have a dog too, a German shepherd."

Scotch and I are members of Gabriel's Angels, an organization that provides pet therapy for abused and at-risk children. Through the Angels we have worked at the Amy Houston School, interacting with seventh graders, trying to build self-esteem and to encourage kindness, empathy, and consideration. We have been involved with programs at two domestic-abuse facilities. At one we worked with children—infants to twelve-year-olds. With the infants and toddlers, Scotch would often lie down to be on the same level with his small fans. Whenever we walked through the door of the room with four- to six-year-olds, kids mobbed us, yelling "Hi, Scotch!" He might go on walks with two or three children, pretend parades through the long hallways. These walks provided a good opportunity for me to commend the children on a job well done and to point out how happy Scotch was to be with them. "Just look how he's wagging his tail!" We would then move on to a group of kids ranging from ages seven to twelve. Often, abused children feel that they have little control over situations, so as a good self-esteem builder I would help these students do obedience exercises with Scotch (sit, stay, come, heel). They also liked to brush his coat and teeth. I often asked them, "What do you like about this dog?" and, "What does this dog like about you?"

Children from abusive situations can find it difficult to think of positive things about themselves. It's a wonderful opportunity to encourage them to recognize their own good qualities.

At the Salvation Army's Elim House we engaged in similar exercises. The kids there taught Scotch to climb the ladder to the slide in their playground. He happily slid down the slide with an impish grin.

We also made numerous visits to Tumbleweed, a facility for homeless teenagers. The kids taught Scotch various tricks, had their pictures taken with him in his Valentine finery, and enjoyed his Santa Dog visit where each one got a stocking filled with teenage treats. These at-risk kids liked to remember their own pets, and they often shared pictures and memories with us. Through Scotch, they learned positive ways of interaction and realized that animals have feelings too. Sixteen of them came to my house for Thanksgiving dinner.

Recently, we have been asked to participate in a new program for juvenile offenders. We have also made special-request visits with the elderly and at a day camp for autistic children.

We have been volunteering at a new Hospice of the Valley facility, a fairly small one, where they take no more than twelve end-of-life patients at any time. The first day Scotch was looking very handsome, groomed by a professional, if you please. When we entered the waiting room area, there was a group of ten people of different ages and generations, all of whom had just lost a loved one. Scotch went around to each person, to lay his head in their laps and offer comfort. Then we moved on to see the patients. We visited for some time with a person who loved dogs; after a while the man in the other bed sat up and invited Scotch to join him. Scotch went over and lay down on a sheet beside the patient, a Native American. He kept stroking Scotch and saying, "This dog has the power." Then he stroked his own head and chest. He cried, and I had tears in my eyes. It was very moving.

Kids and adults alike are drawn to Scotch. He seems to absorb their cares, disappointments, and frustrations. He is always cheerful and happy to see everyone. No matter how many noisy kids or sad people there are, whether we are in a calm or volatile situation, he intuitively knows the best approach. Through this work, our own bond has strengthened. From Scotch I have learned lessons of acceptance and unconditional love. He exemplifies qualities of kindness and compassion that I would like to see reflected in my own life. In the eyes of the children we encounter, we find the face of the future and the chance to make a meaningful contribution.

My retirement years beckon enticingly as a time when we will be able to pursue more opportunities of this nature, allowing a throwaway dog to enhance people's lives by giving generously from a heart full of love.

BRADLEY

—— Ann Rodgers, Retired teacher, happy grandma ——

I lost most of my hearing after the birth of my first son. Gradually, after an autoimmune incident fifteen years ago, I became completely deaf. I tried hearing aids but even the most powerful brought little sound. Eight years ago I had a cochlear implant, which helps somewhat. When my husband died, I realized how vulnerable I was because I could not hear. The implant provides some sound but only on one side of my body, and I don't wear it at night.

While visiting my kids in Seattle a few years ago, I saw a dog on a leash with the words "Dogs For The Deaf." It was my first introduction to a hearing dog. What a great idea! I applied immediately and found myself at the bottom of a long waiting list.

Dogs for the Deaf chooses potential hearing dogs from animal shelters. The dogs are usually small- to medium-sized, under three years old and often mixed breeds. The trainers look for dogs that are healthy, intelligent, energetic, and friendly. Dogs chosen for the program spend four to six months in intensive training. They learn to alert the handler to various sounds such as smoke alarms, doorbells, phones, and kitchen timers. Obedience work is an important part of the process since many people will take

their hearing dog with them everywhere: to work, restaurants, grocery shopping, or on public transportation.

I waited, though not very patiently, for almost two years until Emily Minah, a trainer at Dogs for the Deaf, sent me a picture of Bradley—what a face! To me he looked irresistible. Emily told me that after working with Bradley she had looked at a number of applicants and realized that my situation and needs matched best with this dog's personality, talents, and strengths. I guess it was my lucky day. She found the dog in a rural animal shelter. He was picked up as a stray on the loose. He was very thin. Since he was a medium- to large-sized dog, the chances of someone adopting him were pretty slim. Emily said that she liked his calm gaze. "We often see dogs that give us a look from their kennel in the shelter as if they know who we are and what we do. Bradley gave me that look, almost as if he knew that he wanted to be a hearing dog."

I did all the paperwork, had an interview and a home assessment, and then Emily arrived with Bradley. He was even better than his picture. Emily stayed for several days, giving me a crash course in dog obedience using toys, treats, and play as positive reinforcement. She showed me how to keep Bradley alert to the sound training and how to make the training a lot of fun, to make it a game. She is an excellent teacher and very reassuring. Bradley had no experience of city life. Things like bicycles and motorcycles frightened him. When Emily finally left, I think both Bradley and I were a little nervous. He went into his shell for a while. At first I thought he was just quiet, and I didn't realize how depressed he must have been until a few weeks later when he began to emerge as his exuberant playful self. I started taking him to dog parks to play and socialize.

I am a dog person and have been for most of my life. To have a dog that can be my pet companion and my assistance dog is just awesome. Also, it seems like a win-win situation to rescue a dog and give him a life as a helper and a friend. We are both so lucky and so grateful to Dogs for the Deaf. They are doing important work.

Bradley and I are a good team. He comes to me and jumps at knee level to alert me to many sounds: the phone, the doorbell, the alarm clock. He then leads me to the source of the sound. He recently added an important sound to his repertoire. I take care of my infant granddaughter during the week. At first I was always worried, running back and forth to be sure she was sleeping. It didn't take long before Bradley started coming to fetch me whenever she cried. He figured this out all on his own.

I must keep Bradley alert to the sound work, and we continue to practice obedience. Sometimes it's difficult for Bradley to know the difference between jumping on me to tell me something important, but then not jumping on other people whom he loves. We are involved in an ongoing process, a delightful process. And he really is a keeper, isn't he?

TROOPER

—— Cindy Lipton, Pet Partners program manager,
Animals Benefit Club ——

I already had two young shih tzus, a Tibetan terrier, and a parakeet when I picked up the paper early one morning and saw a color picture of an adorable puppy with a story that broke my heart. A pure-bred shih tzu, six weeks old, had been born with his front leg bones (the ulnas) unattached at the "elbows." The breeder had taken him to every shelter in the city but they were turned away repeatedly until they arrived at a no-kill sanctuary for cats and dogs, the Animals Benefit Club of Arizona (ABC). At ABC, Dee Kotinas, the founder and executive director, agreed to take on the puppy and to be responsible for the anticipated $1700 cost for corrective surgery.

At first I just wanted to make a donation, but then I started thinking about adopting the dog. A little later that morning I raced over to the shelter, met Trooper, fell in love, then went to visit him every day for the next two weeks. After successful introductions to my other dogs, Trooper came home with us—all three pounds of him! Trooper was a special puppy. I think he somehow knew that his breeder's vet and many other people had suggested euthanasia for him. He has always seemed exuberantly happy to be alive. As it turned out, his condition is inop-

erable but he never lets the disability get in his way. He has an outgoing, loving personality and just goes right ahead with life as he finds it.

One day I happened to mention to Dee at ABC that Trooper could be a wonderful inspiration as a therapy dog. When Dee explained to me about the Delta Society Pet Partners program at ABC, I realized that fate must have brought Trooper, ABC, Delta, and me together. ABC adopted the program in 2000 as a way to help people in health-care facilities and special-needs schools with the therapeutic touch of friendly pets. As soon as Trooper turned one, the minimum age for certification, I attended a Pet Partners workshop. A month later Trooper and I passed a skills and aptitude test for Delta certification. We then began a program of orientation that included shadowing working therapy dogs that were currently visiting patients in Children's Rehabilitative Services (CRS) at St. Joseph's Medical Center in Phoenix. CRS is a clinic for chronically ill and disabled children; considering Trooper's size and his disability, it seemed like a good match. Little did I know that the tremendous impact that this eleven-pound dog would have on so many people.

We visit CRS every week. Trooper has a stroller, ("Trooper's Trolley") but he likes to get out frequently to visit. People love to watch him walk and run like a bunny, then stop to sit up like a prairie dog. We go to different areas, sometimes to a maxofacial clinic for children with cleft palates or severely disfiguring birth defects or injuries, sometimes to the clinics for cystic fibrosis or cerebral palsy. I worked for years as a speech and hearing therapist and served seventeen years as an emergency medical technician, so I am comfortable around these young patients with severe disabilities. Trooper never seems bothered by feeding tubes, wheelchairs, ventilators, unpleasant smells, or children making unusual sounds. He is perfectly comfortable being touched by patients with spastic or jerky movements.

We always visit the orthopedic clinic. This area is Trooper's specialty, and he has helped with some exciting breakthroughs. For months we visited a boy we'll call Jason. A brilliant nine-year-old suffering from a crippling disease, who had been through the state system, a boy with a drug-addicted mother and a father who didn't want a disabled son, Jason was clearly mad at everything and everyone. He seemed like a child destined to take out his anger on the world. In the beginning, he never smiled, talked, or acknowledged Trooper's presence in any way. Then one day, as we sat next to him, he surreptitiously petted Trooper

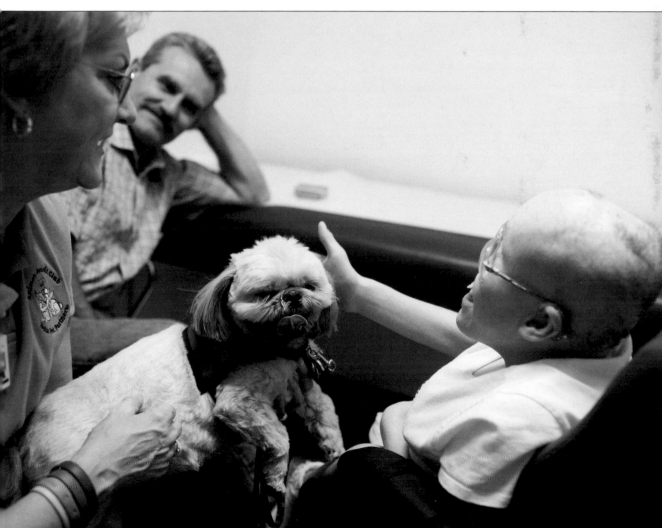

and muttered, practically under his breath, "Cool dog." I saw a small smile at the corners of his mouth. Those two words marked the beginning of a real relationship between Trooper and Jason. The two bonded as Jason asked about Trooper's disability and why it couldn't be "fixed." Later we talked about shih tzus in general, then about spaying and neutering programs, microchipping, the care and cost of a dog, and about our visits to the clinics. As weeks passed, Jason smiled more and more; he started to talk to everyone. By the time he completed the many months of treatment, he had asked his family and his social worker about participating in wheelchair sports at the YMCA. Staff members say that Trooper caused this dramatic change.

Recently we encountered a father who had just been informed by specialists at CRS that his son would never be able to get around without a wheelchair. This news was even more painful because the family doctor had previously assured the parents that the boy would eventually walk. A staff member directed us to a treatment room to visit with the father while his son was X-rayed. The poor man was so dejected that he seemed pulled in, like a turtle. He was gazing down at the floor when we entered the room. He noticed Trooper's way of moving and asked about it. I explained Trooper's condition and then told him about our weekly visits to the hospital. The man began to straighten up. As we talked a little more about Trooper, this father told me that if a disabled little dog could have a job and be a productive member of society, then perhaps there was a place for his son to be productive too. It was as if a fifteen-watt lightbulb suddenly changed to 200 watts. It's amazing to watch people as they make that connection.

And it's not just the patients and families who appreciate Trooper's visits: The staff greets him every week with a chorus of "Trooper's here!" These are people who deal with tough situations all the time, and Trooper provides a bright spot in the day. They practically line up to pet him and welcome him. With so much attention from everyone, typically seventy-five to one hundred people each day, Trooper adores the Wednesday visits! And as for me, I can't wait for Wednesdays to see this special little guy spread comfort and happiness.

MICAH, formerly ALASKA

—— Sue Lavoie, Dog trainer ——

*—— Bob Langendoen, Assistant general manager,
retail building materials supply ——*

Sue: I got a call from a prospective client asking me to work with Alaska, the white German shepherd puppy she and her husband had bought for their son's first birthday. The pup was now jumping up and knocking the baby over. What a surprise! Both owners worked twelve hours a day, six days a week. The wife's mother stayed home with the baby, but she didn't like dogs and didn't want any responsibility for the puppy. When the owners left for work in the morning, he was turned out to wander the neighborhood all day. When they returned home at 9 PM, they put him in a crate in the garage for the night.

On my first visit, Alaska came bounding out of the garage to meet me. What a happy puppy! He was so excited that he wet a little when he greeted me. The family didn't like this expression of excitement and had banned him from the house because of it. My heart ached for this dog—he loved people, but he was neglected by his family for most of the day. As I returned for subsequent sessions, I could see him becoming less and less interested in human contact.

At my first visit both the husband and wife were excited about working with the pup. Subsequent lessons were with the man only. His wife was losing interest. Whenever I arrived for a lesson, it was obvious that I had woken them up. The man would eventually stumble out to the driveway with his coffee mug in hand. He'd listen sleepily as I instructed him in puppy training, but I could see that they had no time to work with the puppy between our lessons. I told him that it wasn't safe to leave a twelve-week-old puppy loose, completely unsupervised while they were at work, but he was not concerned. He said that Alaska just went down the street to play with the neighbor's beagle. Then when the neighborhood kids came home from school, he would romp around the neighborhood with them. At least the dog wasn't totally isolated. Since he was lucky enough not to be run over or stolen, I guess it was good for him to socialize every day with other dogs and kids.

However, at each visit I saw him become less connected with his people and with me. I hated to see him so neglected. I even offered to adopt him, but the owners said he was like their child, and they would miss him if he wasn't there when they came home every day.

One Sunday when I was waiting for Alaska's owners to get out of bed and meet me in the driveway I realized that my heart was breaking over this puppy. I had been trying to help him but, without any help from the owners, my efforts weren't accomplishing much, and it was killing me. I couldn't go there anymore.

In the following months, I occasionally drove by the house looking for signs of Alaska. Now he was chained to a doghouse in the side yard. It was very sad to see him like this. But, to my amazement, a year later the owners called to ask if I still wanted the dog. Their schedule had changed; they were working even longer hours and simply couldn't care for him anymore. My heart leaped for joy. First thing the next morning my husband, Bob, and I drove over to pick him up. The cute puppy I had fallen in love with the first time I saw him was finally on his way to a new life!

Bob: The pup's new life would be quite different. First we gave him a new name, Micah. Then we introduced him to our other dogs, three German shepherds and Mickey, an elderly mutt. The shepherds included Chip; Summer, a young dog that Sue is starting in search-and-rescue (SAR); and Jerry, another white German shepherd, Sue's semi-retired SAR dog. Jerry isn't particularly dog-friendly, so we were prepared to watch him carefully when he and Micah met. To my surprise, Jerry and Micah became friends immediately, almost as if they had known each other all their lives. The others quickly accepted the new guy as part of the pack.

Micah had never lived in a house, and things like slippery floors made him anxious. He remembered and liked Sue, and soon became comfortable with me, but he was very timid around strangers. He had missed out on socialization at an early age when it would have been easier to absorb. He liked other dogs and loved people once he got to know them. The ones he didn't know made him nervous. I have worked in SAR for many years, and I planned to train Micah as my sixth SAR dog. His first official training session was disappointing. I knew he had great potential, but that didn't matter much when he shied away from the team leader who was evaluating him. We had a long way to go.

I took Micah to obedience classes and we hung out at shopping centers to let him overcome his fears. As he became a little more confident, I provided many biscuits for strangers to offer him. We worked toward his Canine Good Citizen test and went to SAR training every week. Slowly he began to come out of his shell. Week after week (sometimes even day by day) I could see improvement, due partly to the growing bond between us, and partly to his important early training with Sue. There was no overnight transformation. A year went by, then two, and I could see that Micah was ready to begin the SAR certification process. The team leader still had her doubts, although she admitted that he was definitely not the same dog we had brought before her two years earlier.

In SAR work, the dog's mission is to find a human in the area being searched. We trained regularly but the process was long and difficult. We'd take a test, and Micah would usually pass it, but he just didn't seem to give it his best. I was perplexed and sometimes frustrated, but I saw something in him that I had never seen in my other dogs. He had a playful nature and a wonderful spirit. I knew that when it came down to it, he knew what he was doing. Maybe he thought I was too serious, and maybe I was. Maybe I would have to start learning from

him how to keep the fun in training. After all, the training is based in play motivation. Maybe I would have to laugh instead of getting uptight.

During a series of tests, some of which we passed and some we failed, I never blamed him. I knew that either I had failed to read him right or that he was trying to show me how he did things in his own way. For better or worse I simply had to trust him, and, especially with a secondhand dog, that isn't always easy. You simply don't know the

dog in the same way that you would know a dog that had been with you all his life. Micah tends to range far on walks. He does the same in field training. I get a little anxious, and then suddenly he will come back to me and lead me to his find—the hidden subject or perhaps a hiker who could be on the trail or 1,800 feet away in the woods! With most dogs you would be delighted if they found someone 200 feet away, but Micah covers a huge range. When he's out of sight, I could go crazy, yelling to call him back, but I have to bite my tongue. After all, I don't want to call him off a scent. Still, it can be a little nerve racking. My biggest fear is that something may happen when he's far away from me: Will I be able to get to him? Will I be able to hear him if he barks? Last weekend he walked into a coyote snare. The cable was tight around his neck, but fortunately he didn't fight it. He just sat down, barking until I came to find him and release it. With his big range, I sometimes get the sense that he'd like to say to me, "You wait here. I'll be back in a while to take you to the rescue." Although he definitely prefers real searches to practice sessions, he generally knows just what to do without help from me.

Human remains detection (cadaver work) is hard for Micah because the search is usually confined to a small area. It's often a crime scene. Getting this dog to slow down, stay nearby, and focus is a real challenge, but he is learning. Recently we did some work for state park rangers who were trying to determine if the site of a 150-year-old graveyard still held human remains even though the gravestones had been removed. We drilled into the soil to allow any residual scent to rise. Then to everyone's amazement, Micah indicated finds time after time as we moved around the area. His alerts were verified by three other experienced dogs, leaving little doubt that bodies were still there. Just imagine: There were bodies that were probably well over a 100 years old, and the dogs could pick up the scent.

Micah makes me humble and proud, and he makes me laugh. I'm his human, and he's my best friend. Throughout my thirty-year career as a volunteer in SAR, I have always been gung ho and serious. Micah keeps me in check. He's my not-so-serious search dog. Whether we are training or on a real search mission, I know that he's out there getting the job done and dragging me along as I wonder what I would ever do without him to show me the way.

Sue: Today, Micah is 110 percent Bob's dog. He likes me, of course, but he really only has eyes for Bob. If Bob's at home, no one else exists.

MARVIN

—— Dr. E.J. Finocchio, Director, Rhode Island SPCA ——

I had sold my equine veterinary practice and become director of the Rhode Island SPCA. My wife and I were enjoying life with no emergencies and no late-night calls. Our son was an adult working in Boston, and we were free to come and go as we pleased. We certainly were not looking for a dog, especially since my wife had been bitten when she was a child. The memory and the fear had stayed with her.

In my new job at the SPCA, the daily routine included a morning walk through

the shelter to visit the dogs and cats and to hand out treats. One day I noticed a black Labrador with almond-colored eyes. It was Marvin. He looked straight at me and then ever so gently took the biscuit I offered. When he was a puppy, Marvin's right hind leg was injured. He can't put any weight on it so he carries it and walks with a limp. His original owners gave him up after three years because they no longer had time for him in their lives, a sad but unfortunately quite common situation. After a few days of shelter rounds, I began to sense that there was something different about this dog, Marvin. I found myself thinking about him. When I talked to my son I happened to mention the dog and he said, "You should adopt him. It would be a good thing to do." But my wife was not at all in favor of the idea so I just continued my morning visits, and eventually a family adopted the dog. They knew at the time that he walked with a limp and that the disability was permanent, but after a few weeks they brought the dog back to the shelter explaining that they were uncomfortable with his lameness.

It just happened that I was in the foyer when Marvin arrived. Our eyes collided again as they had many times before. I stroked his head gently, he pressed his body against my leg and looked up at me. Then he went back to a cage in the kennel.

After a few weeks it became apparent that nobody wanted a lame dog that had been given up twice. In addition there is a phenomenon called black dog syndrome that may have played a role here. People in shelters and rescue organizations have noticed that black dogs are often the last to be adopted if they are adopted at all. They don't photograph well, and in the shelters, for whatever reason, potential adopters tend to pass them by. In some shelters, staff members try to avoid lining up black dogs in cages next to one another; they even put colorful bandanas on the dogs. An organization called Black Pearl Dogs has an interesting Web site explaining this phenomenon and showcasing black dogs.

I wondered what would happen to Marvin and if he would be euthanized. How long do you keep an animal in a cage? Is there a time when it becomes cruel?

Eventually Marvin's turn arrived. He was brought into the quiet room and placed on the table. I held his paw in my hand and was about to insert the needle into his vein when our eyes met once again. As we looked at each other I placed the needle down on the table. From that moment Marvin became my dog forever. I think of him not as a black pearl, exactly, but as my "diamond in the ruff."

His sweet nature and his friendliness made Marvin a natural for therapy work. Five years ago he earned certification with the Delta Society, and since then he has visited many facilities including a children's hospital, several general hospitals, nursing homes, adult daycare centers, group homes, and libraries. He recently received the Delta Society Beyond Limits award. He can perform tricks or just sit companionably next to someone. He puts smiles on the faces of sick children and lonely senior citizens; he brings love and inspiration to many. His story resonates with people who are having a hard time: He knows about loneliness, homelessness, and living with a disability.

Marvin also has a full-time job as mascot and official greeter here at the SPCA. In his honor we started the Marvin Fund to help elderly and disabled people who need food and medical services for their pets. So far the fund has assisted over 1,200 people with many generous donors contributing to the effort. We have raised over $100,000, some of this from sales of Marvin's book, *Marvelous Marvin*, and his Marv Art paintings. To create the artwork, nontoxic watercolor paint is put on Marvin's tail, then, depending on his mood and the wag of his tail, a painting appears.

Marvin has enriched my life by allowing me to help him help those who cannot always help themselves. He is my hero. (And by the way, in case you were wondering, my wife loves Marvin as much as I do. She says she can't imagine life without him.)

KANDU

—— *Ken Rogers, Motor sports consultant* ——

Kandu is an unusual little dog. For one thing, he was born with no front legs. His original owners kept him for three years, but didn't do much with him. Apparently he just slid around on his chest rubbing off all the hair and, from time to time, some skin as well. The owners eventually decided that the dog's quality of life wasn't good enough, or maybe they got tired of caring for him. Who knows? Anyway they took him to be euthanized, but the vet said that the dog had too much heart and was just too full of life, so he turned Kandu over to Evergreen Animal Protective League (EAPL). The people there found a foster home for him and contacted Martin Kaufmnan, founder of OrthoPets adaptive technology. Martin made a padded vest to protect the dog's chest against floors and carpet, and a harness with a roller ball attached.

I saw Kandu on the evening news and told my wife, Melissa, about this amazing little dog. Along with about a hundred other people, we called in to ask about adopting him. When I filled in the long application, I mentioned that our rescued Labrador, Bob, was involved in the Heeling Friends program at the local hospital. Melissa's a nurse, and I'm an EMT. We thought Kandu

would make a cool therapy dog. That idea must have been a plus for us because we were chosen. Kandu came home with us. When Bob, the Lab, first met the little guy, he was so shocked that he jumped right up on a chair. "It looks like a dog, it smells like a dog, but where are the rest of his legs?"

It took a few months for us to get used to Kandu and for him to get used to us. It must have been confusing for him—he had been in three or four foster homes—but eventually everything worked out. The cats accepted him, and he and Bob began to play together. Bob usually lies down to make the playing field more level. Often they play on our bed, Kandu's preferred place because he can easily bounce on Bob to nip his ears and his Achilles tendons. Bob is extremely patient, but when he's had enough, he just lays a paw over Kandu to pin him down. We were initially worried that Bob might be rough, but actually it's the little dog that's the rough one.

Kandu's back legs are very strong. When he wants to get up on the bed or the couch, he just springs up like a grasshopper. He does have a disability but he certainly doesn't think of himself as disabled. Nothing stops him from trying. He gets a little frustrated at times when he can't chase Bob into the underbrush or jump in the water (although he has tried both). I took a neoprene knee brace and made him a vest attached to a frame with roller blade wheels; this apparatus works pretty well on rough ground. We often take walks on dirt roads and trails, and he can run for about a mile. Then we pick him up and put him in a Snugli baby carrier or the baby jogger. He likes to be carried: I guess he has spent a lot of time in that mode, but he also likes to cruise. He has a mono-ski so he can race full tilt down hills and play in the snow. I'm working on a device for the water. Bob retrieves of course, and Kandu really wants to join in.

Melissa says that when people first meet Kandu, they say, "Oh, it's so pitiful! That poor little thing!" But as soon as they see him running along at top speed or flying downhill on his ski, it's, "Wow! Cool dog!"

Once Kandu was comfortable in our home, we started working on the certification process for Heeling Pets. It took about three months to prepare for the various tests. First there is an aptitude test to be sure that the animal is comfortable with strangers and unfamiliar places, and then a

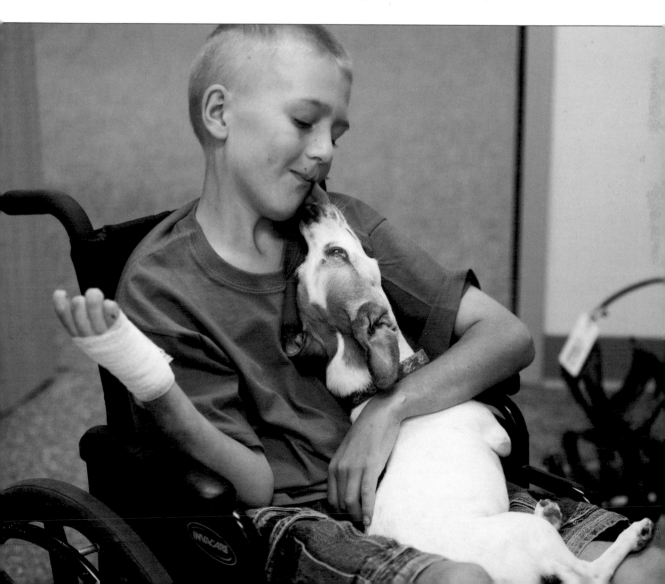

test to demonstrate basic obedience skills. Animals are also tested on their reactions to sudden movements, loud noises, wheelchairs zipping by, people yelling, and falling objects crashing to the floor. The animals must be low key, friendly, patient, and quiet.

Handlers go through two tests, one of which is scored on how they handle the animal in different scenarios including crisis situations. Handlers must show that they are in control of the animal at all times. The other test is to demonstrate strong people skills. Kandu is really smart, and very, very motivated by treats, so he picks up on things quickly. At the tests he charmed everyone and scored pretty well all around; I guess I did O.K. because we were dually certified to start visiting patients at the Yampa Valley Medical Center. In Heeling Friends you make a commitment for two years with a minimum of two visits each month.

Kandu just loves it. When we drive into the hospital parking lot, he gets all excited. I put his wheels on, and he cruises down the corridors, his roller blade wheels flashing little lights. Staff members, visitors, and patients all stop to say hello. This dog has got such great spirit that it seems to be infectious. When visiting patients, we only go to rooms where the staff and the patient have invited us. I always ask the patient if he or she is ready for a visit and if they are allergic to dogs. Then, if everything is O.K., I put a clean sheet on the bed for Kandu. Once he gets calmed down, which usually takes less than a minute, he's happy to hang out. If he's on your bed, he'll be spooning you. When he's on a bed or in a lap I take his wheels off so he's more comfortable. Dogs can be a real icebreaker. Many patients like to talk about Kandu and about their own pets. Hospitals can seem intimidating. Sometimes patients are worried and frightened, but our visits can make the hospital experience a little less traumatic.

In addition to seeing patients in their rooms, we often stop by the physical therapy area. Recently we have been spending time there with ten-year-old Tyler, one of Kandu's favorite people. Last summer, Tyler lost his feet and parts of some fingers from an illness. The first time we met, Tyler asked all about Kandu and held the little dog on his lap. Kandu snuggled down and would have happily stayed there all day. Tyler stroked him with a big smile. His mom said she hadn't seen the boy smile for weeks. Kandu is full of energy but at the same time he likes to be held, and he really likes Tyler.

Recently we went to Los Angeles for the Nuts for Mutts dog show. Kandu won Best Kisser, Best Physically Challenged, and finally, Best in Show. He definitely is the best, and I think "his" patients would all agree.

HERO, formerly BANDIT

—— *Ralph Diner, Medical psychologist* ——

Hero had a rough patch. Staff at the Huntington County Humane Shelter in Indiana came to work one morning and found a dog tied to the door with a note saying, "This is Bandit. We can't keep him, please find a good home for him." The person who tied him up and drove off either didn't like him much or loved him greatly. What could make someone tie a dog with no ID to the pound door in the middle of the night? Did he do something unforgivable?

Had someone died? Been born? Or had they discovered his hip dysplasia but could not afford the repair? There is no doubt Bandit must have been wondering what had happened in his life.

The shelter posted his story online and advertised in local papers, but no one stepped up, and his time was limited. The head of the shelter liked him; she let him sleep by her desk all day. She decided to contact MidAmerica Border Collie Rescue for help.

They arranged to send him to a foster home in Wisconsin. There, Grace Saalsaa, a very kind woman, gave him a new name, Hero. Grace kept him for four months until I came along. After my dear yellow Lab, Sinbad, died, I spent three months looking for the right dog. I looked in ever increasing radii until I saw Hero's eyes on MABC Rescue's Web site. My vet and my brother both agreed that from the photo he was definitely my dog: a deep, old-soul type.

I knew he had the soul of a therapy dog. Grace was not so sure: She wanted me to be certain I would love him even if it turned out that he was not cut out for that sort of work. After a rigorous interview with MidAmerica, I managed to convince them that I would be a good "forever dad." Once again, Hero got into a crate and was loaded on a plane, this time with a T-shirt of mine that I had worn jogging so he would recognize me when he arrived in L.A. Well, let me tell you, the T-shirt worked. When they wheeled him out, he had his eyes locked on me.

We immediately began training, and Hero, who started out resource guarding, turned into one big, giant, gentle smile. He's a sensitive guy who reaches out to me and others. He finally believes that people actually like him. At first he used to look at me as if to say, "Is it all right for me to let others love me? Will you abandon me?" My theory has always been that the more love a dog can get or give, the better. Hero has sunk into this life as if it were a hot tub for his soul.

Last year, we helped set up a dog therapy program for the local Vitas Hospice. For our work they gave Hero and me a rubber chicken luncheon where we each received a rubber chicken, not to mention awards from the mayor of L.A., several state senators, and other government dignitaries.

We now work primarily at Vitas Hospice, at an L.A. Veterans Administration clinic, and with residents at the Ararat Nursing Facility. I have found that a sympathetic dog can make patients more receptive to psychological treatment so Hero helps with my own private patients as well.

We participated in Crisis Response efforts during Firestorm 2007, visiting firefighters and others affected by the terrible fires in southern California. We were invited to go to Blacksburg, Virginia, after the fatal shootings at Virginia Tech in 2007. For two weeks we counseled students, faculty members, and their families and other survivors. Hero provided comfort and helped people open up with me in grief and healing processes. We worked many long days, much more than usual, and it was grueling for both of us. After the first week, I managed to take a day off, and we went to a state forest where Hero could just run without his vest and be a dog. With the vest on, he knows he's working, and he's an angel. When I take it off, he's ready to play and tear around like any dog.

Hero has helped many people—he actually is a hero. And he loves the work. Sinbad, my Lab, used to whine and pace in the car for twenty minutes on the way to Malibu to swim. Hero does the same thing when he knows he's near the Hospice or an old people's home.

COOPER, formerly BARNEY

—— *Donna Francis, Teacher for the deaf* ——

Barney, a young Labrador, abandoned and alone, wandered the streets until he finally ended up in the yard of an older couple. They took him in and tried to care for him as best they could, but the wife was not in good health and her husband had his hands full taking care of her. Although the dog was extremely sweet and friendly, he seemed stubborn. He had a hard time learning things. In addition, he had demodectic mange and an ear infection. The kindly couple wanted what was best for the dog, but they knew that they were not the best family to provide a home for him, so they surrendered him to Lone Star Lab Rescue.

The rescue group's vet treated the mange and the ear infection. Then Barney, this loving yet very goofy Lab, went to a foster

home to recuperate and learn how to live in a house as part of a family. Foster care involves housebreaking and obedience training for good manners. Once again, Barney had trouble learning; he didn't respond to praise or correction. He seemed stubborn, even stupid. Then finally one day people at the rescue group realized that the dog was deaf. Working with hand signals was the best way—indeed the only way—to train him.

I was a fairly new volunteer as a foster home provider but I did have an extensive background in dog training. Also, I was a teacher for the deaf and fluent in sign language. I took several deep breaths and agreed to take on the challenge, even though I had never trained a deaf dog before.

In my house foster dogs were always kept separate from my own dogs for an initial quarantine period. They slept crated in another room at night. Well, this simply did not work for Barney. Either I or one of my dogs had to be within sight at all times, and when I thought about it, I realized that this was perfectly reasonable for a deaf dog. After all, if I put Barney in a separate room, I had essentially blinded him since he couldn't see what was going on in the family pack, and of course he couldn't hear what was going on either. As long as Barney could see one of us, he would stay calmly in his crate. If not, well, I'm sure my neighbors thought I was torturing him before I figured out what he was trying to tell me. I moved his crate into my bedroom where he could see someone at all times, and he was content.

When he was out of the crate and sleeping near me, I learned to wake him before I left the room or I would face a panicky Labrador running frantically from room to room in search of me. When he

did something he shouldn't, perhaps chew a book or the remote control, I had to go and get him—no yelling from the comfort of my chair. At night he learned to come in from the backyard when I flicked the porch light on and off. After observing my senior dachshund ring a bell on the doorknob to go out, he began to do the same. I used sign language and other hand signals with him constantly. At the same time I spoke to him verbally to make my facial expressions and emotions easier for him to read. I took him to obedience classes. Now, I'm not going to lie and say it was easy. It wasn't easy. He learned early on that if he didn't want to do what I asked, all he had to do was turn his head away so he couldn't "hear" my command. (Occasionally some of my human students use the same tactic.) He loved to chew, and almost anything would do: books, magazines, computer discs, remote controls, and the cordless phone. Barney could counter surf with the best of them. Once he even tried to jump into the kitchen sink to get at some dirty dishes.

I worked with Barney intensively for two months, and it was amazing how quickly he learned. He changed from a confused and frustrated dog to one that was eager to please and eager to learn. Each day he seemed to say, "So what new sign are you going to teach me today?" And he would say it with a wagging tail and a huge grin. Day by day, he wiggled and wagged himself right into my heart. I decided to make him a permanent part of my family. I adopted him and changed his name to Cooper.

One of my other dogs, Jett, a rescued poodle, was a certified therapy dog. Jett accompanied me to school and worked with my students. I thought perhaps Cooper, with his disability, could be effective in the program. I worked on basic manners and taught him American Sign Language. My students followed his progress eagerly, anxious for him to be able to come to school. They were delighted when he earned his Canine Good Citizen title. Two months later Cooper was ready for his big therapy dog certification test. He passed with flying colors. He was ready to be a therapy dog working with deaf children.

As an itinerant teacher, I travel, to different schools. On his first day of classes, Cooper and I set off to a junior high school where I worked with a hearing-impaired student. Cooper walked into the school like a pro, loving all the attention he got from teachers and students in the halls, but when it was time to work with the student, he was attentive and calm. Next, we went on to the elementary school where I worked in a special education classroom with a deaf student and his hearing classmates. The students ranged from mildly to severely challenged, some with multiple problems. These children had been working all year with my other dog, Jett, and they were eager to meet Cooper.

Cooper walked into the room with me and went straight over to a child (we'll call him R) who was lying on a beanbag on the floor. This boy had been unresponsive to most of our attempts to communicate with him, even ignoring Jett. Well, Cooper lay down on the beanbag next to R and wriggled right up to him. R giggled and reached out to pet the dog. With a huge smile, he continued to stroke Cooper. The teacher watched in amazement as the two lay there for a long while until eventually Cooper decided it was time to move on to another child. There were seven students in the class, and Cooper worked the whole room. He went from child to child, sometimes sitting quietly for petting, sometimes

lying on the floor while the children lay next to him and loved all over him. He even tried to work with one of the teacher's assistants, a woman who was scared of dogs. The adults in the room started asking how I had trained him to go from child to child, each time seeming to know how the child wanted to interact with him. I had to tell them that there was no way in the world to train a dog to do that; it was just instinct. Cooper was a natural therapy dog.

Then we went to my office where I expected Cooper to nap for a couple of hours. Jett is always exhausted after working with the children, but Cooper seemed to be energized. He didn't nap. He wanted to greet everyone who came to the office. In the afternoon, we moved on to another elementary school to work with a sixth-grade hearing-impaired student. This girl was used to doing her class work with me while Jett usually napped and relaxed. Once again Cooper definitely didn't want to nap. He was glad to show the student just how much sign language he knew. She was happy to communicate with him in this way and fascinated to see that he was deaf, just like she was.

Therapy work can be hard on dogs. A dog should not work all day, and I always try to ensure that my dogs get numerous breaks and downtime. When we finally went home I expected Cooper to be exhausted, but he wanted to play with the other dogs and go on our usual walk with my nieces. Working actually seemed to give him more energy. After that first day I was relieved to see him settle down to a more normal schedule of work and naps.

Cooper loves to go to school with me. He responds to commands in sign language, and the students get a big kick out of working with a dog that speaks their language. They often write about him and will write much more if it's about Cooper and not just some boring writing assignment. Most of them love to read dog books, and their interest in Cooper has prompted them to do research on dogs and responsible pet ownership. A dog in the classroom provides a relaxed atmosphere in contrast to the stress that hearing-impaired students often feel at school. They can read to Cooper and he listens with his heart as his ears don't work, and he never criticizes or corrects their pronunciation. He also provides an effective reward system: Good work and good behavior can mean free time with Cooper—a walk down the hall with him, a chance to give him a biscuit or take him outside to go potty (yes, they actually consider this a reward!). For an extra special reward, Cooper might even get to come to school an extra day.

I knew Cooper would be a good therapy dog, but I didn't realize just how great he would be. He's a natural with good instincts. He has helped many children. A boy who was very reluctant to use sign language finally began to do so in order to get Cooper to respond to his commands. A deaf girl, one of Cooper's longtime friends, said recently, "I love Cooper because he's deaf like me, and sweet."

OPIE

—— Judith Anderson-Wright, Certified pet dog trainer ——

Opie had seven different homes in seven years. At three months he was an adorable Jack Russell terrier, a Christmas present; at six months he ate a $3,000 leather couch and his exasperated owners sent him to the shelter. From there he went in and out of a couple of homes with people who didn't understand the needs of a terrier, which include lots of exercise, lots of attention, and lots of obedience work. With the fourth family, Opie managed to chew his way through a door. He spent the next three months living on the street. I guess he's a pretty good ratter.

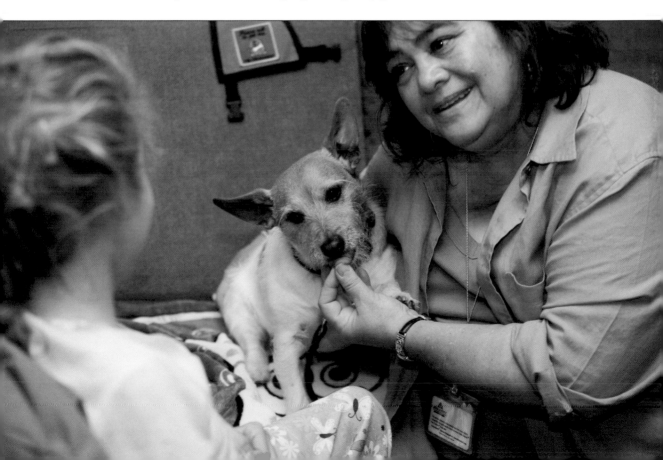

After that he went to a home with kids and a cattle dog. Apparently the dog tried to herd Opie and the kids, while Opie tried to herd the kids and the dog. It must have been chaotic, to say the least, and Opie found himself back in the shelter. Then for two years he lived with a family where everyone worked outside the home. He spent fourteen hours a day crated so when they came home he went crazy. He also had seizures and pretty severe separation anxiety. After consultation with the vet, everyone decided that rehoming was probably the best option.

When I first met Opie at the vet's office, he was bright-eyed and seemed eager to please. He definitely needed someone who understood Jack Russells and someone with a great deal of patience. I thought he also needed a job. Since I am a lover of all terrier breeds and it seemed to me that this dog deserved a better chance, the match was made right away. I love him dearly, but I must admit the care and training of Opie was not always easy. He had incredible separation anxiety and hated being placed in a crate. If I left him alone for more than five minutes, he would have a frenzied breakdown, complete with trembling, barking, and sometimes even fear-induced urination.

Slowly we began to develop a close relationship based on leadership and mutual respect. We had a lot of help along the way. My business partner took Opie to her house whenever he needed a respite from life with my already established pack of four dogs. We worked our way through challenges with advice from animal behaviorists and trainers. Our wonderful vet, Dr. Elise Thomas-Holt, advised on correct medication and good nutrition. Opie has benefited from traditional treatment and from herbal medicines. As his stress level declined, he had fewer seizures.

Opie and I have created a wonderful partnership over the past three years. Even now he still has a smidgen of separation anxiety, but he certainly has come a long way. He is a fast and enthusiastic learner, and he seems to thrive on human contact. He tends to greet everyone with a wagging tail and often offers tricks to get people to pay attention to him. I wrote a dog-bite prevention program for children called Operation Opie. Together we have educated nearly 1,000 children about safe ways to meet and interact with dogs. Opie serves as an effective teacher as he happily allows children to approach him and pet him. He is head counselor and mascot at Great Dog Camp K-9 for Kids, where children ages six to eleven learn how to interact with dogs and to train dogs. They also learn about humane treatment for all animals.

With his delightful Jack Russell terrier personality, his intelligence, and his love for humans, Opie has touched the lives of many people. He visits nursing homes, hospitals, shelters, schools, retirement centers, hospice providers, prisons, and mental health facilities. One day he was in a special-education classroom visiting quietly with a young woman who had not spoken for months, when she suddenly said, "Opie, Opie." He did a quick spin in front of her while she gave him a huge smile. At a retirement center a very ill elderly woman told me that Opie was an angel if she ever knew one. In a shelter for victims of abuse and domestic violence, Opie gives families, especially children, a sense of normalcy in a world where they have been forced to flee their homes, sometimes leaving beloved pets behind. In a nursing home, he used to snuggle up next to a woman with terminal cancer who told him that he made her feel the best she ever felt.

Opie is one of a group of rescued dogs that work in Healing Species, an exciting violence intervention program for children. Rescued dogs—dogs nobody wanted—act as helpers and teachers. Each class begins with the dog's story of abuse and neglect. Opie was bounced around from one home to another. No one understood him; often people got angry and yelled at him or hit him. Many children can relate to Opie's story of rejection and neglect. They make a connection and feel empathy for Opie, an important step in avoiding a path of abusive behavior. In this highly successful program, children learn how to remove themselves from all forms of abuse or violence, how to grieve and manage their anger, how to find respect and compassion for the feelings of others, and finally, how to give love.

Opie is eleven now. He shows no signs of slowing down, but I know that he is not going to be able to keep this pace up forever. My only regret is that we have been together just a short four years. I sometimes wonder what this little guy could have done if we had paired up sooner. However I do like to think that those difficult seven years were not a total waste. Opie's story has resonated with children and adults. It helps people to know that Opie was persistent, willing to change, and eventually able to trust as he entered his seventh home in seven years.

Some of my favorite visits take place at a Ronald McDonald House where families and patients can stay while the children are undergoing treatment in a nearby hospital. Some children are there for a long time, some we only see once or twice, but most of them (and their parents) seem to brighten up as soon as Opie appears. He modulates his behavior according to the patient's needs. Sometimes he just lies quietly and cuddles, happy to be there, and sometimes the children hide treats around the room so he can search for them. The kids think he is quite remarkable to be able to find all the treats, and Opie thinks it's a pretty good game.

CORDIAL GRACE, BATMAN, and CARMEN

—— *Billie Peters, Greyhound rescuer* ——

Cordial is a beautiful red fawn female greyhound. She had a successful racing career at the Daytona track in Florida. When she retired, an elderly couple adopted her. We understand that the gentleman had a heart problem that required oxygen, and he would walk the dog with his tank tagging along. When he died, Cordial was returned to the kennel at the track. I'm involved with All-Star Greyhound Rescue in Lafayette, Indiana, so through the grapevine I heard about Cordial's plight and her depression upon returning to life in a cage. She came north on the next trailer of dogs headed for their forever homes. At the age of seven and a half, she arrived in Indianapolis and then moved in with us. Because my husband and I are in our eighties ourselves, we adopt the senior dogs that are harder to place.

I had two therapy dogs before Cordial so I started gradually working with her to prepare for the certification test. It was slow at first but once she understood what I wanted, the progress was rapid. She's a very smart girl and had no trouble at all passing the test. She loves dressing up in her jeweled collar for visits.

In our four years as a therapy team, we have visited nursing homes, hospital geriatric wards, a drug rehab hospital, a developmental school, and a veterans' home. Cordial is one of the gentlest dogs I have ever been around. She really shines with elderly and disabled patients as she's happy to stand still and let them pet her. Her height is handy for wheelchairs and beds. These people's days get kind of glum sometimes, so she's a good distraction for them.

We participate in reading programs for children at two local libraries. Cordial listens patiently while a child reads aloud, then we give the reader a bookmark picture of Cordial inscribed "Reading with Cordial." She is a good listener and popular with the children.

We have another greyhound, Batman, a large, brindle nine-year-old, also a certified therapy dog. Batman raced in Wisconsin but was not very speedy; thus he had a short career. He was adopted twice. However, when the mom in his second home died suddenly, her husband and sister became so stressed with their loss and taking care of other pets that they returned Batman to All-Star Greyhounds. From there, he came to our home. Batman takes turns with Cordial for visits, though she is more experienced. What Batman lacks in experience he makes up in friendliness and tail wagging. He's my big handsome boy.

We go to most of the facilities once a month, twice a month to the veterans' home. Both dogs love to visit. As soon as I say, "Let's go to work!" they're so happy they do that little play pounce.

The newest member of the pack is Carmen. She lived with a family for a while, but I guess the mom just couldn't cope. She told her children that the dog ran away. We think Carmen was on the streets at least two weeks when the shelter picked her up. When they didn't get a response from the dog's original adoption group, they called All-Star Greyhounds. Our director asked for

a volunteer to meet the shelter lady halfway, so my husband, Bill, and I drove over and picked up Carmen just north of Indianapolis. Because she was skin and bones with a bad case of diarrhea, no one wanted to adopt her, and we now had a foster girl. A few months later someone was interested in her, but Bill said, "No! She's my dog now."

She just recently passed her testing and will be a tremendous Pet Partner. She's affectionate and loving, a real Velcro dog, who doesn't want to budge as long as she is being petted. These three seniors should work well. They can take turns, each visiting the facility where their personalities best fit the residents.

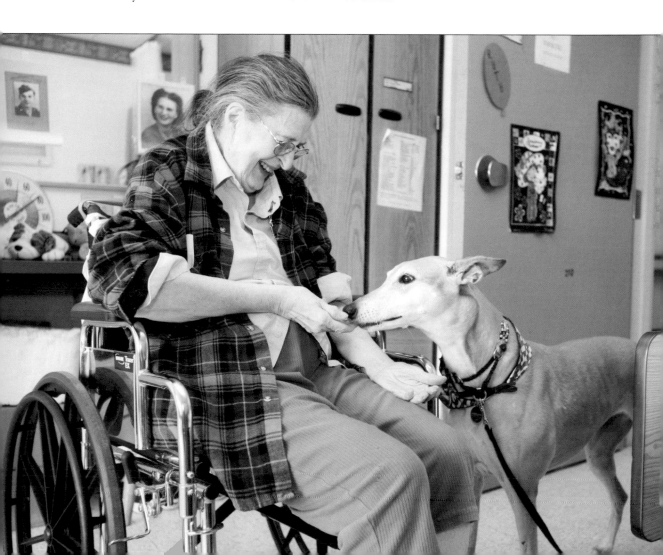

SHAKESPEARE

—— Jennifer Alfonso, Anger management consultant, animal advocate ——

I adopted my black Labrador mix, Shakespeare, from a Labrador rescue group when he was about seven months old. I don't know much about his background except that he had been an outdoor dog, definitely neglected, possibly abused. His original name was Fang. I had been fostering dogs for some time, but when I met Shakespeare it was instant love. He was gentle and sweet, and best of all he seemed very interested in pleasing me. From the beginning, he tried to do whatever I asked, sometimes guessing if I didn't make it clear enough. Once, when I pointed at the dog crate, wanting him to get into it, he jumped on top of it instead. He is very vocal. He actually tries to talk to me when he is frustrated, happy, or just plain wants something. He mimics human speech: He says quite clearly, "I love you," "how are you," "hello," and "happy birthday." My all time favorite: When you ask what the cow says, he MOOs.

When Shakespeare came to live with me I was working with the Washington, D.C. Humane Society Humane Education program, SPEAK (Sharing Positive Experiences Animals and Kids). I brought my dogs into inner city classrooms to teach children about caring for dogs in hopes of increasing empathy for all creatures. Many of the children were afraid of dogs or viewed them as objects to keep outside or use in dogfights. Shakespeare was an instant hit. His "talking" ability catches everyone's attention, but I am especially impressed by the way he captures the hearts of children who are afraid of dogs. These children seem to respond to his gentle nature and eagerness to please. When Shakespeare meets young children, he immediately lies down and slowly crawls toward them as if he knows that his sixty-pound size might be intimidating.

In the classroom we talk about animal care, then the children practice training Shakespeare. They give him commands, and he usually complies. If the weather is nice, the kids run with him behind the school and throw tennis balls for him. We sometimes hide his toys in lockers and watch him open the lockers to search for them. He often sings with the kids. If invited, he will sit on the teacher's lap. At some point during most visits we sit in a circle on the floor; each child holds a treat out low, and Shakespeare walks around the circle gently taking the treats. There is always a lot of interaction, and Shakespeare thrives on it. I'm impressed

to see children who start out fearful and then after a few visits will examine his feet and even touch his teeth.

Our work with the Humane Society was featured in a *Washington Post* article in 2005. For some time with National Capitol Therapy Dogs we visited children and oncology patients in a local hospital. Now we continue to volunteer with the Humane Society humane education program and with Therapy Dogs International. Shakespeare's current certifications include the American Kennel Club's Canine Good Citizen program, READ (a program designed to help children learn to read by reading aloud to animals), and Therapy Dogs International. As a team we participate in flyball, an

international sport where dogs take part in a relay race competing against other teams. Shakespeare holds a Flyball Champion Gold title. He serves as an ambassador for animals in his volunteer work.

He manages to touch the hearts of people who don't want to get close to other people. As an anger management counselor, I sometimes bring Shakespeare to work with me. Often people who have a hard time talking find it easier to speak about their issues while petting him. I run two anger management groups for teenagers at a group home where some of the teens report that they only come to group because of Shakespeare. He has an uncanny ability to connect with adolescents who are going through a hard time.

A client once said, "Shakespeare is the only person who loves me." At the same home I facilitate a pet therapy group where the kids work on clicker training; they have taught Shakespeare commands such as "high five," "crawl," and "take a bow." Many teens report this as the highlight of their week.

When I was clinical director at a therapeutic high school, Shakespeare and my other dogs went to work with me every day. The students were all on behavioral plans, and many would choose time with Shakespeare as their reward for following the rules. One of the students had a pervasive developmental disorder. When upset, he would bang his head on his desk. If a staff member tried to redirect him, he would just keep banging, but if I brought Shakespeare over, the dog would whimper for attention and the banging would stop immediately as the boy reached his hand out to touch Shakespeare.

Shakespeare adds a color to my world that was previously missing. With him, I am able to see more and appreciate more. I have many wonderful letters from children who have worked with Shakespeare. Here are a few excerpts with the original spelling:

"I got a dog and I care for my dog like my best friend Shakespeare. I don't kick my dog."

"I feel bad for pets and other animals that are being treated mean. I really, really like the way you teached us about animals."

"I learned that you have to be patients. Now I know how to be calm, loving, and caring."

"I should always be friendly, but when you see a dog tide up, call the Humane Society. Animals can't talk, you can."

SOPHIE

—— *Don Conkling, Veterinarian* ——

Sophie spent the first three years of her life as a street dog in Mexico City. She was guarding three puppies, all dead, when she was picked up and taken to the Refugio San Franciscano. The Refugio, home for 1,700 dogs mostly running loose, and a number of cats, is run by a remarkable eighty-one-year-old woman, Ita Martinez de Escobar de Osomo. Ita started this sanctuary years ago. It's a tough place but filled with love. Ita can tell you the name and history of just about every animal there.

Soon after Sophie's arrival, Christi Payne from Compassion Without Borders came to talk to Ita about taking a few friendly, adoptable dogs to California where various rescue groups would find homes for them. Sophie, always interested in people, was hanging around when Christi came to choose the first group. Sophie and nine other dogs headed north. As a vet, I work with several of the rescue organizations, so Sophie came to the clinic with two other dogs that needed medical treatment.

I fell in love with Sophie immediately. Brenda, my wife, took just a few minutes longer. The little Mexican street dog came home with us that night, howling all the way. She was shy at first but she has a true terrier's

grit. She did well in obedience classes and then started agility training, but she would leave the course to go visit anyone on the sidelines who had ever given her a cookie. One of the trainers, who had therapy dogs herself, said, "I know something this dog would like to do." So six months and two days after she arrived in our lives, Sophie and I were certified as Delta Society Pet Partners. Since then I have become an evaluator for Delta as well.

Sophie comes to work with us at the veterinary hospital every day. Even though we work full time, we always manage between three and six visits each week. Hospice is our favorite. One patient who was paralyzed in all but one hand loved dogs so much, she would have her caregiver wheel her out to a nearby trail so she could visit with passing dogs. We were a novice team at that point, and it was very rewarding to see the peaceful expression on the woman's face as Sophie snuggled with her. At one visit, the patient was so uncomfortable she had not slept for several days, but as soon as Sophie settled down next to her, she fell asleep almost immediately, though even asleep, she kept stroking Sophie with one finger. An hour and a half went by, the woman slept, and Sophie

barely moved a muscle. When we left, she dragged me down to the trail, expressing herself quite plainly, "After all that, I've got to move!"

Another patient had trouble swallowing, which caused her to gag and make sounds that could be scary for a little dog but not stalwart Sophie. Whenever we visited, the patient wrapped herself around the dog and the two napped together for an hour or so. Then there is the patient with dementia who thinks that Sophie is her dog. Even when her memory is most clouded, she remembers Sophie's name, although she doesn't remember mine. And there is Dorothy who, at ninety-four, is very sharp, and one of our favorite people. Sophie is always happy to see Dorothy and would be happy to see her even without the pound cake. She jumps right up on the couch and proceeds to show off her reading skills. I hold out a flash card that says "Bang!" and she flops over on her side. She can read a number of words, but she's sharpest on "Sit up," "Shake," and "Bang!" We have been visiting Dorothy for over a year, and we haven't missed a single week. When you meet someone you really click with, it seems as if you have known them forever. Dorothy often says, "Sophie is my best friend."

We also visit the psychiatric unit at Stanford Hospital. This is an interesting population, so there is always something new. The young girls with anorexia are some of the saddest to see, and also some of Sophie's favorites. They are there for a while, then they go home and a month or so later they are back, worse than before. One day we met a patient who felt compelled to cut himself. At first I was a little nervous about him, but he was a sad, gentle soul. He lay down on the floor, rested his head against Sophie, and petted her for a long time. Sometimes just being there with someone is Sophie's most important job. We try to help the patients think of better things and work on appropriate ways to interact. To tell you the truth, I think the staff benefits as much from our visits as the patients do. Sophie is a comfort to everyone because she is so loving, yet she makes no demands, except occasionally, "Please go on petting me."

VOLKL

—— *Joe Hurlburt, Professional ski patroller, craftsman* ——

—— *Deb Hurlburt, Professional gardener, hobby farmer, volunteer* ——

Deb: People know that Joe and I have a weakness for German shepherds so we tend to get calls when there's one without a home. One day my friend Krissi was on the phone. "Have you gone by the shelter lately? They have a four-month-old shepherd puppy there. He's a cute little thing with enormous ears, so sweet. You'll see him there in a big cage all by himself."

Well, there are some dogs that need you and some dogs that you need. We really needed this puppy. In less than a year we had lost Jackson and then Cassidy, two beloved German shepherds, and we were feeling a little lost ourselves. I went to see the puppy and fell in love immediately—it would have been hard not to! Our oldest shepherd, Tracks, was with me and he seemed to approve. I begged the shelter staff to hold the puppy for me just long enough so I could go to the place where Joe was working to tell him. Joe said, "If you really want to do this, let's get him!" So we brought him home and named him Volkl after our favorite skis.

Some cowboy had won this pup in a card game. He left the dog home alone all day and came back to a torn-up house. The cowboy decided that he had a bad dog and took him to the shelter. At least the guy realized that the dog needed a different home. And it was certainly our lucky day.

We had adopted most of our dogs as adults so it had been a long time since we had a puppy. It was quite a challenge. Volkl just didn't know anything. We had four other dogs: Walter, a big, fluffy mutt; two German shepherds, Tracks who was ten and Cedar, eight (we think); and Rosie, queen of the pack, weighing in at twelve pounds. We have no idea how old Rosie is, but we know she's pretty tough because she survived a bobcat attack. She was torn up so badly that we didn't know if she would survive. She had over one hundred stitches and drains everywhere. But she recovered to continue ruling over us all.

Volkl's best playmate was Cedar, a dog who had come to us at six. He had been in three different situations before finding us. He spent the first four years of his life in a fenced backyard before he was dropped off at the kill shelter. Then he went to two different homes in two years, and when I met him, he was close to being sent back

to the shelter again. All his life he had been so misunderstood that he had serious trust issues. The poor dog had had very little socialization, and the contacts he did have with people were often not good ones. One of his previous owners had misused an electric collar while trying to "train" him. I knew that he wanted to be a good dog; he just didn't know how, and he took himself way too seriously. Cedar had been in our home for about two months when Volkl arrived. At four months Volkl didn't take *anything* seriously! He helped Cedar see that life could be fun and playful and that there was no need to be uptight all the time. In turn Cedar taught Volkl how to swim.

We did some basic obedience work with Volkl and found him intelligent and eager to learn, eager to please. From the beginning we played hide and seek games everywhere, including in the snow, and he was definitely interested. Joe works on the ski patrol at Grand Targhee. We both helped out with training the search dogs there. I'm pretty good as a volunteer victim.

Joe: After Volkl passed an on-hill obedience test, I started taking him to work with me and training him with the avalanche dogs. He passed his Level 1 Avalanche test so he is certified for avalanche work. We will go for Level 2 later this month. In addition to that, we are training Volkl for wilderness search and building search. We don't get much call for building search around here, but it's fun to train in so we do it. Volkl should test out in wilderness search this spring. Recently we started him on cadaver scent. When he's searching, we want him to alert whether he finds a live person or a dead one. He just has so much drive. He really loves the game, and he's only three!

I worked in regular search and rescue for many years, but Volkl led me into canine search. For his early training we continued playing hide and seek, then started with runaways. Deb would take Volkl's favorite toy and run off with it while I held his leash. At first she hid right where he could see her, then gradually we made the hunt more difficult and substituted different people for "victims." Someone would hide while Volkl was still in the truck and couldn't see where the person had gone. Someone might even go the site to hide before we arrived. When Volkl made a find, we always celebrated by playing with him using the toy for a tug game. In the beginning I stayed very close to him to be ready for the game. Soon he realized that he had to bring me to the person he had found before play with his toy could begin. He indicates an alert by jumping up on me. He only jumps up when he's alerting, never just for fun. We chose this signal because he does it naturally—and

with a lot of enthusiasm! You really want to reinforce the enthusiasm. Manners are good, but you must be careful not to discipline the play drive out of a dog. Volkl has so much drive. When he makes a find and comes back to jump on me, he may return a number of times if I'm slow getting to the person. When we're working in the dark, he goes back and forth to make sure I can see him.

Volkl qualified to go to Canada for a weeklong training course with the Canadian Avalanche Rescue Dog Association (CARDA). We'll go up there with Jason O'Neill and his dog, Murphy. Jason runs our dog program at Grand Targhee so Volkl and Murphy often train together. They're good friends but they get pretty competitive when they're both digging for the same boot or mitten.

Deb: We're having a lot of fun with Volkl and we're very proud of him, but if it had turned out that he wasn't a good search dog, we would have been perfectly happy just to have him as a pet. He is a good dog. He's really a reflection of all the good dogs we have had before he came along, the good dogs that trained us.

BYRON

—— Rachel Wright, Pet Partners program coordinator ——

When Lillie, my eighteen-year-old cat died, my husband and I decided to go to the Humane Society. And there was Byron, a small black puppy curled up in a little ball. He looked at me with those big brown eyes, and I said to my husband, "That's the dog we've been looking for." We took him home with us. He was shy and timid, about four months old, a flat-coated retriever with separation anxiety and other complications. He had been abandoned in a local park. I don't know anything about his life before us, but he has managed to overcome whatever it was. He began by rescuing me from the sadness I felt after losing Lillie.

After we completed a number of obedience classes, I attended a Delta Society Pet Partners training workshop and then signed

up for some therapy dog classes with Byron. We were certified as a team when he was just over a year,

My other rescued dog, Mia, a basset/lab mix, assists me in my private practice as a substance abuse counselor. I am program coordinator for the Delta Society Pet Partners and a team evaluator for potential pet partners. My work seems like a dream come true. I feel blessed to be at the other end of the leash with Byron and Mia. I am grateful to them and admire the way they enthusiastically and faithfully give so much to humans despite the fact that humans initially did not do this for them. I have always been impressed by the willingness to forgive that we often see in rescued dogs. We humans sure have a great deal to learn from them.

Every week, Byron and I visit patients at the Bailey-Boushay House, a very special place for patients living with AIDS and other life-threatening illnesses. Staff and volunteers there work hard to create a sense of normalcy for people, many of whom feel lonely and perhaps no longer have family, friends, or even a place to call home. Many have experienced rejection and abandonment. Pet therapy is an important part of this caring atmosphere. When Byron visits patients, they know that he's happy to see them and that he loves them.

For two years we visited a particular patient, a man who loved dogs and shared a special bond with Byron. The first time we met this man he had just learned that one of his own dogs had passed away. He invited Byron to lie beside him on the bed while he showed me pictures and reminisced to Byron about all the animals he had known in his life. Each subsequent visit followed the same pattern.

One day, before we had even reached his room, the man came out in his wheelchair in tears. He said, "I'm so glad you're here! I've been waiting for you. My father died this morning, and I need you, Byron. I really need some dog love." Byron went over to the wheelchair and put his head on the patient's lap. We stayed for a long time that day as the man cried and talked about the bittersweet relationship he had with his father. When we left, he said, "Thank you, this has meant so much to me. I don't know what I would have done without the two of you here today." Several weeks later this man passed away, and Byron and I both grieved for him. For the next few visits, Byron always stopped at the man's door. He would look up and stare at me.

I am happy that we were able to be with this man during a very difficult time in his life. This is a memory I treasure because I know that Byron made such a difference.

GRACIE

—— *MaryAnn Griffin, Director of Aging and Adult Services,*
City of Alexandria, Virginia ——

After the death of my beloved dog, Fred Griffin, I began a search for a new canine friend. I checked Petfinder.com and then went down to the Washington Animal Rescue League (WARL) to see a cute little dog featured on the Web site. WARL is a no-kill shelter that aims to save dogs that can potentially be adopted. They often take dogs from other shelters where their chances for adoption are slim. Well, the dog I had come to see was cute indeed, but in the next cage I spotted a lovely dog with soulful eyes and a beautiful face, a dog that was missing her right rear leg. I left the shelter

that day without making any decisions, but all that week I kept seeing the dog's face in my mind. I returned for another look and couldn't walk away.

The dog's story was a sad one. She had come to WARL from a shelter in West Virginia where she'd been slated for euthanasia. The staff there thought that she had probably been caught in a trap. When she arrived at WARL her leg was badly mangled and infected, and had to be amputated it.

In the next few weeks I completed the adoption process. When I came in to pick up the dog, the veterinarian told me about the harrowing surgery and how they had almost lost her on the operating table. When he asked me if I had chosen a name, I told him that I was considering Cassie or Gracie. He responded, "Well, given the grace with which she came through the surgery, I think Gracie would be a fitting name."

Gracie easily made the transition from life on the streets to sleeping on a Laura Ashley comforter. She is very popular in our neighborhood; everyone knows the three-legged dog. Gracie likes other dogs and loves all people. When we go for a walk the neighborhood children call her by name and run out to play with her. They are fascinated by the fact that she has only three legs: They all want to know what happened to her. Gracie's disability really has not limited her in any way. She runs like the wind and is the happiest dog I have ever met.

About a year after I adopted her, Gracie and I went through the orientation for People Animals Love (PAL) an organization whose mission is "to bring people and animals together, brightening the lives of the lonely, easing the pain of the sick and enriching the lives of at-risk children." When a volunteer from WARL learned that Gracie was a PAL dog, they decided to feature her on the cover of their newsletter. As a result we were invited to visit at Walter Reed Hospital, where so many soldiers are returning from the Iraq War with the loss of arms and legs. That day we met with a number of these brave people. They enjoyed Gracie, and she loved them! This visit prompted PAL to feature Gracie on the cover of their newsletter with the headline "Amazing Gracie," so my girl enjoyed some celebrity status for a time.

Gracie and I visit the Arleigh Burke Pavilion nursing home where a number of the residents have had strokes and are unable to speak clearly. We time our visits to coincide with the end of lunch so there is always quite a crowd seated in the common area. You should see the way so many residents, otherwise noncommunicative, manage a smile and an expression of joy when the dogs appear. One resident often calls out, "Where's Gracie?" There are five to seven dogs in our group; some are small enough to be put in people's laps, and some of the larger dogs are just wheelchair height so it makes petting them easier. Gracie is medium-sized, and of course she can't stand up on her hind legs to be petted, but somehow we always manage. She has amazingly soft velvet ears, and the residents enjoy stroking them. The staff and those residents who are alert and verbal seem especially drawn to her. People are interested in her story and sympathetic because she has only three legs.

Gracie spreads happiness wherever she goes, among nursing home residents in wheelchairs who enjoy her visits and to neighborhood children who delight in throwing sticks for her. They all love Gracie, and I do too.

SADIE

—— Alisa Armijo, Insurance agency owner ——

Some years ago, when I was working as a news anchor and reporter at a TV station in Midland, Texas, I was sent out to investigate the alarming euthanasia rate at our local animal services bureau. The facility welcomed us in hopes that the story would educate area residents who just did not grasp the importance of spaying and neutering their pets. A staff person led the cameraman and me to a cage with the first dog scheduled to be euthanized that morning. The dog had actually been on the table the day before but the animal control worker on duty didn't have the heart to put her down after the dog had wrapped her paw around the woman's arm. This particular dog had been found wandering around the local college campus, sharing lunch with students near the duck

pond. As I peered into the dark cage, I encountered the saddest eyes I've ever seen. They belonged to a very small, very thin, and very dirty golden retriever. She looked as if she wanted to say, "Are you here to take me home?" That was it for me! I was living in a small apartment and had no intention of getting a pet, but I was a goner the minute I looked into those eyes.

That very evening we ran the story, and Sadie appeared on TV for the first time. The response was so overwhelming that the animal control center teamed up with our station to sponsor a "Pet of the Week" segment for our morning show, a feature that is still in place today. A local veterinarian offered to spay or neuter animals adopted through the program—for free! Hundreds of animals have been adopted because Sadie put a face to the problem.

During our first year together Sadie got up with me every day at 3:00 AM. She slept under the news desk as I read the morning news. She greeted our in-studio guests, went to appearances with me, and often accompanied our weatherman for live shots in the field. I realized that she was no ordinary dog. She loved everyone: children, the elderly, people of every shape and color. A year later, we became a certified therapy team. For several years we worked in eldercare facilities. Sadie is used to older people and people with disabilities. There are lots of walkers and wheelchairs in our house at Thanksgiving and throughout the rest of the year.

Now we visit with one- and two-year-olds at Homeward Bound, a transitional living center for mothers and children from shelter programs. Some are homeless, some come from domestic violence situations. When we first started with the one-year-olds, Sadie quickly formed a bond with a bright-eyed girl. The child absolutely loved Sadie but the only way she knew to touch the dog seemed to be hitting, either with her hand or with an object. We began to teach her to pet Sadie softly, and after some improvement, I taught her how to use a brush to groom the dog. After she learned to be gentle we noticed that the little girl began teaching others in the class how to pet Sadie correctly. Now she always acts as Sadie's guardian during classroom visits, showing great concern for her friend's safety and comfort.

Some children immediately take an interest in Sadie, while others ignore her. One little boy we'll call Jeffrey showed no interest in her until the day that Sadie brought in her favorite toy, an old tennis ball. After watching the dog retrieve the ball several times, Jeffrey approached her with a ball from the classroom toy box. When Sadie leaned forward and gently took the ball from his hand, it was as if a lightbulb had turned on inside the boy. In short order he had a pile of balls, all sizes and colors, at Sadie's feet. Each time he handed one to her, she gently lifted the ball from his hand and placed it on the floor. It sounds like a small thing, but I will never forget the expression on that child's face! They formed a bond that day that they still share.

Sadie seems to have a sixth sense about people. I'm often amazed at her ability to know what a child needs. When the kids are upbeat and ready to play, she's ready too. If a little one is afraid, she will turn her back to the child, somehow knowing that her back may be less frightening than her face. She will wait patiently, sometimes for months, for a child to get over the fear of being near her. Her early experience with hardship as a stray may have taught her to recognize emotion and pain in others. I love helping people realize the untapped potential we can find in rescued animals.

MARLEE

—— *Karen Lanz, Veterinarian* ——

Marlee came to us in the spring of 2006 after Hope, our fifteen-year-old German shorthair pointer, died. Hope was a dear companion and a nursing home visitor extraordinaire. My then husband, Otto, and I, along with our two cats and miniature dachshund, Zonker, were lost without her. Otto had told me about Marlee when she came into the veterinary teaching hospital where he practices. A group of vet students had found the dog at our local pound. She had a partially amputated right foreleg. The

remaining portion of the leg was infected and in dire need of attention. Surgery was required and, if left at the shelter, the dog would surely have been euthanized. The school has a rescue fund program for cases like this, and therefore students often check out area shelters looking for dogs that need help. In this case they adopted Marlee and brought her to the hospital.

Otto performed the full amputation. I am a vet, too, and we had seen many dogs and cats learn to accommodate to a missing

limb and go on to live a full and happy life. After the surgery a student volunteered to foster the dog. One day, when we were talking about how much we missed Hope, Otto said, "Why don't you just come meet Marlee?" Well, you know how that goes. Of course we brought her home. She fit right into our household and became fast friends with Zonker. After about two months she realized that this was really her home, and she just blossomed.

She's very athletic: She can hike two miles on her three legs, and I am often amazed at her agility. She can run so fast after a tennis ball that we don't play ball when the grass is wet because I'm afraid she could slip and hurt herself while racing at top speed. She's crazy for tennis balls but so smart I can tell her that this is the last one I'm throwing. She will chase that ball, then head for the house.

Marlee's sweet, gentle nature made me realize immediately that she would make a wonderful therapy dog. After a little fine tuning at local obedience classes, we were ready. Several months after she joined our family, Marlee and I became registered Delta Society Pet Partners. We began with a hospital and nursing home visiting program called Paws With Love. Soon my brother-in-law, who is a lieutenant colonel in the Army Reserve, suggested that Marlee's status as an amputee could make her a welcome addition to the therapy dogs visiting at Walter Reed Army Medical Center. I contacted People Animals Love (PAL) and was fortunate enough to join their group on visits to Walter Reed. Marlee was well received at the hospital, and I think she was a source of inspiration for some of the brave veterans who are returning from the Iraq War with missing limbs and other disabilities. Guys in wheelchairs marked "Purple Heart Combat Wounded" would say to this little dog, "I know what you're going through."

Recently we visited the outpatient physical therapy facility where veterans are working on recovery, many of them learning to use prosthetic limbs. As we walked around the room stopping to chat with people who were interested in the dogs, Marlee hopped up on a large bench beside a soldier taking a break from working out without his prosthetic legs. We talked a little, he asked about her missing leg, and petted her for a while. Another veteran in a wheel chair joined in, and Marlee was in heaven with one guy rubbing her ears and neck and another stroking her belly— three happy faces. It occurred to me that day that since people with disabilities often have others doing things for them, the fact that they were giving this dog such obvious pleasure had to be very gratifying. Looking around that room full of heroes I felt privileged to be there and to do anything we can to make their time just a little bit easier.

Marlee and I have now moved to Kentucky so we only get to Walter Reed occasionally when visiting family in the area. When we do go there, we are part of the American Red Cross Pet Therapy Team at Walter Reed, a great group. In Kentucky we volunteer with a group called Wonderful Animals Giving Support (WAGS). We work at the local hospital in physical therapy and are also involved with a program where children read to dogs. Marlee likes everyone, but she responds especially well to kids.

I will always be grateful to the students who saw potential in a badly injured dog and rescued her. Marlee has been a joy every day.

IVORY

—— *Jay McLaughlin, Rehabilitation counselor* ——

Several years ago I provided a foster home for various dogs in an effort to help out Animal Adoption and Rescue Foundation (AARF), our local adoption/rescue group. During that time many dogs arrived, stayed for a while, and eventually moved on to good permanent homes. Then along came Ivory, this husky or malamute or whatever he is, with one floppy ear, and I knew we would be together for the duration.

When he was about a year old, Ivory was rescued from a situation where he'd been left tied up outside in all weather with no shelter. He ended up at AARF and came to my house for foster care. At first he was so spooked you couldn't raise your hand above your head without him fleeing under a table or behind a couch. We tried for weeks to get him adopted, with no luck. In time he calmed down, and we became great friends. We both love the cold, we like to swim, and we love to meet new people. I don't know exactly what made me decide to keep him— we got along really well from the beginning, the stars seemed to line up, and I could not possibly be any happier or more fortunate.

I was a student in the Rehabilitation Counseling program at the Medical College of Virginia (MCV). For one of my classes I had to do a presentation on alternative therapies, so I did some research on animal-assisted therapy. I discovered that MCV actually has a pet therapy program, Paws for Health. Thinking I could add some depth to my presentation if I had some experience in the field, I applied to the Paws program.

Ivory had to be evaluated for health, temperament, and behavior. He passed the temperament and behavior tests with flying colors, but in the health exam he tested positive for heartworm. This was a surprise for everyone since he had previously tested negative many times and had been taking heartworm preventative medication for years.

As soon as the heartworm treatment was successfully completed, we went to the MCV Children's Medical Center for our first pet therapy visit. First we saw patients in the general pediatric unit: some in their rooms, and some in the Nintendo Room where I was happy to see that many kids were actually more interested in Ivory than they were in the video games. As we walked from room to room, a five-year-old girl named Timmy escorted us, boosting Ivory's stamina with a steady supply of sour cream and onion Pringles. Then our other escort, a staff person, asked us to go to the Pediatric

Intensive Care Unit (PICU) to visit a young girl just out of open heart surgery. She was very weak with a transparent oxygen mask over her face. She couldn't really talk, but when she motioned that she would like to see Ivory a little closer, I moved him next to the bed where, with a little coaxing, he put his paws on a towel and rested his head next to her. She petted him, then gave him her first postsurgery smile.

I'm not a highly emotional person, but that was an overwhelming experience. When I told the staff that this was our first visit, they were amazed. They said Ivory acted as if he'd been doing this work all his life. That day we were signed up to return for regular visits with the children. Soon we were also seeing a group of visually impaired adults at the senior center and a group of residents with cognitive impairments, mainly

Alzheimer's, at a retirement community. On our first visit to the retirement community, one very old lady with advanced dementia petted Ivory, then started crying. He just stood next to her and laid his head on her lap for about five minutes. His instincts amaze me; I try to watch him and follow his lead.

The places we visit are different with diverse populations, but many of the benefits are the same. Whether on a pediatric floor or an Alzheimer's unit, the day can be long and boring. A good pet visit breaks that monotony, distracts people from things that are bothering them, and generally makes the setting seem more normal. The words "sterile" and "hospital" fit together perfectly, but "sterile" is usually the farthest thing from a person's mind when he thinks "dog"—especially when that dog sheds like mine does! Even with the shedding, Ivory is very clean. He has a bath before each visit.

It's good for children and adults, and for patients and staff, to see a friendly dog, to touch something soft and warm and alive. Of course pet therapy's not just for patients. One day when we arrived at the children's medical center, we found the child life coordinator waiting for us. She asked us to go straight to pediatric ICU. A child had passed away there a short time before, and she knew the staff could really use a visit with Ivory.

Several months later we were invited to work with patients hospitalized for psychiatric reasons. As the first session began there were ten adults in the dayroom, men and women ranging in age from about thirty to seventy. Ivory went up to a young man crouched in a chair, head down, arms wrapped around his knees. He ignored Ivory. He obviously wasn't interested in anything and that included petting this nosy dog.

Ivory continued walking around the room. Some people started petting him and talking to him. Typically he spends a few minutes with one person, then moves on to another. I noticed the guy in the chair uncurling a little bit and watching Ivory out of the corner of his eye. Ivory wandered back over to him, and this time the man actually reached out and started petting him. When Ivory's standing in front of you, one ear up and one ear down, tail waving back and forth, he's kind of hard to resist. Then the man actually started talking, a real surprise for all of us. He talked a little to Ivory, a little to the other people, reminiscing about things.

Ivory kept walking around, and you could feel the atmosphere in the room warming up. After half an hour or so, one of the therapists commented that everyone in the room was smiling, something no one had been doing when we arrived. That was about the time when they asked if we would consider coming in on a regular basis.

Over the years I have tried to emulate Ivory's best characteristics and make them my own. It's not always easy. Once we were in the pediatric ICU visiting a teen-aged girl. She was really, really big and bloated, probably due to medications, some of which can produce severe weight gain. Her hair was greasy and matted, her skin was horrible, her face slack, dull, and uninterested. I've been seeing kids in the PICU for ten years now, and even with the really sick ones, even in a coma or something, you can tell that they're normally happy, healthy kids who are just in a tough spot. This girl was not like that. She looked like she'd never been happy; she looked like she'd never been cared for. Ivory, of course, went straight up to her bed and shoved his nose up to greet her. When she reached out to pet him, I saw that her hand had six fingers. I have always fancied myself an open-minded and poised person, accepting differences in people and taking things as they come. And on the surface I was that person, making friendly conversation with this girl just like I do with everybody. But I was faking it; she didn't know that, but I did. Ivory was most definitely not faking it—he was as genuine, real, and present as one being could ever be with another. He would have stayed all day.

I thought about it for the rest of our visit, the whole way home and all that day, and I still think about it. I realized that I had to raise the level of my compassion, care, and empathy to be equal with a dog. With a dog—not with Gandhi, or Nelson Mandela, but with a dog. That was an immensely powerful lesson for me.

I am undeniably a better human being as a result of the years I've spent with Ivory. He's an incredible animal, and I'm just so happy I've been able to have this time with him. There will certainly never be another Ivory. He's probably only got a couple of years left here with me, but he has changed the course of the rest of my life.

Adopting a Dog

DO YOU *REALLY* WANT A DOG? A few questions to consider:

1. **What exactly are you looking for in a dog?**

   If you are looking for companionship, are you seeking a partner for long walks, or for sitting together on the sofa, for company in the office, for strenuous hikes in the mountains—for all of the above or none of the above? Would you like a dog to work with, perhaps in animal-assisted therapy or agility trials or search and rescue? How do you see a dog sharing your life?

2. **How will a dog actually fit into your life?**

   Realistically, how much time do you have to devote to care, exercise, grooming, and training? Do you travel? What will you do about vacations? Dogs need companionship: They are social creatures, pack animals, not stuffed toys to cuddle with when you are in the mood and to ignore the rest of the time. A dog that does not get enough attention will be an unhappy dog and probably a nuisance as well. If you work all day, leave your dog at home alone, and have classes, meetings, and social events in the evenings, you might want to consider adopting a cat. Some cats are quite content to have the house to themselves during a major part of the day as long as they are fed well and given attention when they demand it. If you

have a fairly sedentary lifestyle or if you are away long hours, consider an older dog, not just an adult dog but actually an older dog. These mature sweeties have usually settled down and may demand less of your time.

3. **Are you looking for a dog to be a companion and playmate for a dog that you already have?**

   This can be tricky. Often a dog with "too much energy" is not getting enough attention from his human companion. Adding another dog to the family can make the situation worse. Never bring two new dogs or puppies into your life at the same time. They will bond to one another, and you will be peripheral at best. If you do already have a dog and decide to get another, one of the opposite sex and of roughly equal size is usually the best choice.

4. **Are you looking for a dog of a specific breed?**

   Try not to be seduced simply on the basis of looks. Consider temperament, activity, size, and especially what that particular breed is designed to do. Hunting dogs may retrieve anything that is not tied down, and they are apt to roam if unsupervised. Some herding dogs have such an intense desire to work that they need a job or at least an owner who is prepared to spend time training them and giving them an occupation, whether it be herding, agility trials, or something else. Otherwise these dogs will find jobs for themselves and this may involve chasing cars.

Be aware that some breeds have a predisposition to medical problems such as hip dysplasia, deafness, seizures, or various forms of cancer.

Learn about different breeds and what you can expect from them. This knowledge can be useful in evaluating mixed breed dogs as well as purebreds. Talk to dog owners, trainers, vets, and shelter personnel. Educate yourself. Read.

5. **When to adopt?**
This is highly variable and depends on your individual situation. The busy holidays are not a good time to bring a new pet into your home and into your life. Never give a friend a pet as a surprise; it often ends badly for the pet.

6. **Can you afford a dog?**
Try to anticipate, at least in a general way, the expense involved in training classes (don't economize here—it's the best possible investment), boarding if you travel, providing good-quality dog food, and of course medical costs. Even a young, healthy dog needs immunizations and may have an accident or injury.

HOW TO START A SEARCH FOR THE DOG OF YOUR DREAMS

Once you have evaluated your situation, decided that you do want to look for a dog, and have a sense of what kind of a dog you would like, what next?

1. Some veterinarians place homeless animals. Often, dog trainers know of available dogs and can be helpful working with a dog that you decide to adopt.

2. Shelters, sadly, are usually full of candidates for adoption. Check out large municipal shelters and private ones, both large and small.

3. There may be individuals in your neighborhood who work in an informal way to place homeless animals.

4. Check the Internet. Petfinder.com is a good resource. Also try searching "pet adoption," "dog adoption," "animal shelters," etc.

5. If you are interested in a specific breed, contact the American Kennel Club for information on rescue groups for that breed. Dogs with breed rescue groups are usually placed in foster homes. The person fostering the dog can be a valuable resource for you. He or she has had an opportunity to observe the dog and usually is familiar with the characteristics of the breed. Remember that purebred dogs do turn up at shelters as well.

6. Do not be surprised if the shelter or rescue group requires interviews, extensive questionnaires, references, and/or home visits. A good rescue organization will be as selective about turning over a dog to you as a good breeder would be.

TIPS FOR GOING "JUST TO LOOK" AT A SHELTER, A VETERINARIAN'S, OR A FOSTER HOME

1. **Talk with the people caring for the animals.** Explain what you are looking for. Ask about the dog's history and temperament. If you sense that they don't have time for this or are trying to talk you into taking an animal

simply because it needs a home ("If you don't adopt her, she'll be euthanized tomorrow"), go somewhere else. Responsible people in the business of placing animals understand the importance of making a good match. After all, they are the ones who see the sad results of decisions made on impulses such as, "What a cute puppy! Wouldn't it be fun to have one!"

2. **Consider an adult dog.** A puppy can be a surprise package. An adult dog may give you a better sense of how he will turn out, though of course you must allow for temporary depression or overexcitement caused by stress.

3. **Do not bring children, especially young ones, with you to help choose a dog.** It is a sure route to an impulse choice that you may regret later. Wait until you have a good idea of the dog you think is best for your family, then bring the children in to see how they and the dog interact.

4. **Do not take a dog simply because you feel sorry for the poor thing.** With any luck the dog you adopt may be with you for ten or fifteen years, perhaps longer, and it is just as important for the dog's sake as it is for yours that the relationship be a happy and successful one.

5. **Visit the dog several times before making a decision.** Take her for walks if possible. Notice how she responds to other dogs and to people. If you feel at all unsure, go to other shelters and look at other dogs.

6. **Hire a good professional dog trainer for a consultation and evaluation of the dog you are considering.** Ask the trainer to consider your needs and your situation. This may seem expensive but in addition to taking your dog to obedience classes, it is the best investment you could possibly make, one that will pay off throughout the dog's lifetime. Temperament testing can be helpful. Many shelters and rescue groups can give you the results of DNA tests. The dog's breed (or breeds) will offer you clues about what to expect.

7. **Bring family members and possibly other pets to meet a dog that you are seriously considering.** This is an exception to number 3: In this case you are bringing children to meet a specific dog, not presenting them with the option of any dog at the shelter. If you have cats or other pets, you will want a dog that doesn't chase or, even worse, injure or kill them.

8. **Take your time.** Adopting a dog is an important decision and a major commitment. Talk it over with people whom you respect, especially people who have had experience with dogs. Think about it. Sleep on it.

BRINGING YOUR NEW DOG HOME

Plan ahead

1. **Make an appointment for a veterinary checkup for your new dog as soon as possible.** Plan to bring records of any known immunizations as well as a stool sample. You may also want to schedule an appointment with a groomer.

2. **Shop for supplies: A dog crate** of an appropriate size with a comfortable, washable bed will give your dog a den of his own, a place where he will be safe. If he is in a crate, he cannot chew electric cords or deposit puddles around the house. Do not leave the dog

in the crate for long hours during the day. Use common sense.

Dog food to which the dog has been accustomed will make the transition to a new home easier and stomach upsets less likely. If you decide to switch foods, do so gradually—substitute a little more of the new food each day. Discuss quality dog food with your vet and/or the staff at a good pet products store.

Bowls for food and water.

Toys that are safe to chew are important for teething and for entertainment. Toys stuffed with your dog's kibble, peanut butter, or small treats are great entertainment when the dog is in his crate.

A collar with a name tag (your address and phone number), a leash and a long line.

3. **Dog-proof your home as much as possible.** Remove potentially dangerous objects as well as things that could be damaged. Designate an area where the dog can comfortably spend time with you. Do not give a new dog the run of the house.

4. **Decide with your family or roommates what the rules are to be.** This way you can all help the dog learn from the very beginning. Consistency is extremely important.

THE BIG DAY

You fill out the adoption forms, pay the fees, and take your new dog home with you. It is an exciting experience, the beginning of a new relationship.

1. **Introduce family members and pets in a controlled way.** Keep the atmosphere calm and quiet. Never leave a new dog unsupervised with children or with other pets until you have a good sense of the dog's potential reaction, not to mention the reaction of the child or pet in residence. Gaining this knowledge will take weeks or longer, not days. Children must be supervised and taught to be gentle with animals, for their own sake as well as the animals'.

2. **Use the crate.** This will help with house training and avoid other destructive behavior. Remember, prevention is often the best training. Feeding the dog in her crate and leaving her there with kibble-stuffed toys can make this den more appealing. Do not reward barking, scratching, or whining by letting the dog out of the crate. Wait until she is quiet. Be sure that she goes out to relieve herself often enough so that you know she is not yelling, "Emergency!"

3. **Spend as much time as you can with your dog, especially in the beginning.** Plan to bring the dog home over a weekend or, better still, during a vacation. During this time occasionally leave the dog alone in the crate for short periods so it can learn that your departure does not mean abandonment.

4. **Be patient.** Remember that your dog has been through some stressful, perhaps even traumatic, experiences and will need time to settle down and to learn what you expect. Leave a leash or a long line on the dog in the house so that you can easily call him to you-don't forget treats when he reaches you! Keep a bag of something delicious in your pocket at all times.

5. **Look for professional help right at the beginning.** Sign up for classes.

Prevention is the watchword: Set your dog up to succeed. Try to anticipate his actions in order to avoid letting him make mistakes. Orchestrate situations so that you can say, "Good dog!" rather than "Bad dog!" Be prompt and generous with compliments and rewards for good behavior. Use a positive approach; your dog will learn quickly and easily.

6. **Exercise is important.** Both you and the dog will feel better and probably behave better as well. Check with your vet for the appropriate level of exercise. You can overdo it, especially with puppies, older dogs, dogs with physical problems, or dogs that have been leading a sedentary life. Start out slowly, use common sense, and take your cues from the dog. Remember, most dogs are eager to please and will overtire without complaining.

7. **Enroll the dog in an obedience class.** This involves an investment of time and money that will really pay off in the long run. It can make all the difference in helping a dog become a great companion.

Do some careful research before choosing a trainer. Ask friends who have had successful experiences with obedience classes. If possible, attend a class as an observer. You should be comfortable with the training methods and the way the trainer treats students, both human and canine. A trainer who kicks or hits a dog or suspends one by the collar is a trainer to avoid. A good trainer will understand the importance of tailoring all training to the individual. Methods that might be effective with a dominant, strong-minded dog would not be appropriate for a more submissive, timid dog. Sometimes second-hand dogs have had bad experiences with humans, making them fearful and insecure. Training based on positive reinforcement usually works best, and in my experience it's a lot more fun.

Your job is to learn how to best motivate your dog. A trainer can be a valuable ally in your efforts to include your dog in your life. A well-behaved, socialized dog can visit friends with you, travel with you, share vacations, and perhaps even accompany you to work.

There are many good books on dog training. (See Recommended Reading.) They are most effective when used in conjunction with actual classes.

Work with your dog, include this dog in your life, and above all, enjoy your dog!

As a writer points out, "He is your friend, your partner, your defender, your dog. You are his life, his love, his leader. He will be yours, faithful and true, to the last beat of his heart. You owe it to him to be worthy of such devotion."

To Get Involved

If you think you might like to do therapy work with your dog, there are some important considerations. First, ask yourself: "Will my dog enjoy this work?" "Will he or she be comfortable meeting strangers?" "Does my dog enjoy being touched by people outside my immediate family and close friends?" "Can my dog tolerate stressful situations?" Of course, in therapy visits you will be with the dog, and you will be vigilant about protecting him, but the fact remains that some dogs are more suited to therapy work than others. Many evaluators have told me about dogs brought to them for certification testing, dogs that are clearly uncomfortable around strangers, wheelchairs, loud voices, and other unexpected noises. These dogs usually have a handler who is excited about the prospect of being involved in therapy work and who somehow manages to ignore the fact that the dog is really not at all enthusiastic. So try to be realistic about your dog's aptitude for the job.

If you decide to go forward, check around your area to learn where dog visits are accepted and which organization handles the certification process for the facility you prefer. There are many groups, large and small. Among the most well-known are the Delta Society, Therapy Dogs International (TDI), Therapy Dogs Inc., and the Good Dog Foundation. All four organizations offer training programs for animals and their handlers, as well as testing and certification. Most will assist the handler in locating an appropriate facility to visit, and will usually provide backup support once visits have commenced. Delta registers many different species of animals—cats, rabbits, guinea pigs, birds, horses, etc., in addition to dogs. The Good Dog Foundation operates currently in New York, New Jersey, and Connecticut, though they are planning to expand in the future. There are many small, local pet therapy groups but most of them are affiliated with one of the larger groups for training and certification.

You and your dog will be considered as a team. Your dog must be well-socialized and competent in basic obedience before you even sign up for a training program. Once in the program you and the dog will go through testing, training, and more testing. Then you may be asked to do further work on certain challenges and return for another try, or you may receive certification then and there. Your certification will usually indicate which populations your team will be allowed to visit. High-stress situations such as some mental health facilities and groups of active, unpredictable small children are not appropriate for every dog, or for every handler. These restrictions are for your own good and for the welfare of your dog. Often there may be opportunities to work in more suitable situations. You want to have pleasant, gratifying visits and, above all, you want your dog to enjoy the work.

Together you can truly make a difference in people's lives. You can bring distraction and fun into an otherwise dreary day. You can comfort a sad, frightened person in a hospital. You can bring a smile to the face of a sick child or a lonely senior citizen.

Good for you, and good luck!

Activities to Share and Organizations of Interest

GENERAL

The American Kennel Club
www.akc.org (212) 696-8200
The AKC can provide information on clubs involved in many different activities, such as agility, obedience, AKC Rally, herding, lure coursing, and tracking.

The United Kennel Club
www.ukcdogs.com
The UKC can provide information on many different activities including agility and obedience trials. Mixed breed dogs that are neutered/spayed may participate.

AGILITY COMPETITION

United States Dog Agility Association
www.usdaa.com

North American Agility Dog Council
www.nadac.com

Canine Performance Events, Inc.
www.k9cpe.com

CAMPS

Attending camp with your dog can provide good shared experiences and lots of fun. There are many good camps; a few are listed below.

Camp Gone to the Dogs
http://camp-gone-tothe-dogs.com

Camp Barking Hills
www.campbarkinghills.com

Glen Highland Farms Canine Outdoor Adventures
www.highlandvue.com

FREESTYLE COMPETITION

Canine Freestyle Federation
www.canine-freestyle.org

Musical Dog Sport Association
www.musicaldogsport.org

OBEDIENCE COMPETITION

The American Mixed Breed Obedience Registration (also agility and other activities)
www.ambor.us

Association of Pet Dog Trainers
www.adpt.com

American Kennel Club Canine Good Citizen test
www.akc.org/events/cgc/index.cfm

American Kennel Club Rally
www.akc.org/events/rally/index.cfm

PET-ASSISTED THERAPY

Angel on a Leash
www.angelonaleash.org

Center for Human-Animal Interaction, VCU School of Medicine
www.chai.vcu.edu

The Delta Society
www.deltasociety.org

Gabriel's Angels
pet therapy for abused and at-risk children
www.gabrielsangels.org

The Good Dog Foundation
www.thegooddogfoundation.org

Healing Species
www.healingspecies.org

Heeling Friends
www.heelingfriends.com

HOPE Crisis Response
www.hopecrisisresponse.org

National Capital Therapy Dogs
www.nctdinc.org

Pet Assisted Wellness at Stanford (PAWS)
www.stanfordhospital.com/forPatients/
patientServices/pawsGuestServices

People, Animals, Love (PAL)
www.peopleanimalslove.com

Reading Education Assistance Dogs (READ)
www.therapyanimals.org/read/about.html

Reading with Rover
www.readingwithrover.org

St. Vincent's Animal-Assisted Therapy
www.svcmc.org/body.cfm?id=1519

Therapy Dogs Inc.
www.therapydogs.com

Therapy Dogs International
www.tdi-dog.org

Therapy dogs at Walter Reed Army Hospital
(see article, www2.redcross.org/article
/0,1072,0_312_7481,00.html and video,
youtube.com video, www.youtube.com/watch?v
=kt2kAPPl5v0&feature=PlayList&p=CDC3BA6
3AEB30136&playnext=1&index=11)

Wonderful Animals Giving Support (WAGS)
www.kywags.org/KYWAGS/about_wags.html

SEARCH AND RESCUE

The American Rescue Dog Association (ARDA)
www.ardainc.org

Canadian Avalanche Dog Association
www.carda.bc.ca

Search Dog Foundation (SDF)
www.searchdogfoundation.org/98/html/index
.html

SERVICE

The Assistance Dog Institute
www.assistancedog.org

Dogs For the Deaf
www.dogsforthedeaf.org

For Better Independence Assistance Dogs
www.forbetterindependence.org

Happy Tails Service Dogs
www.happytailsservicedogs.com

The Hearing Dog Program
www.hearingdog.org

Hearing and Service Dogs of Minnesota
www.hsdm.org

Paws with a Cause
www.pawswithacause.org

SHELTERS AND DOG RESCUE

All-Star Greyhounds
www.allstargreyhounds.org

*Animal Adoption and Rescue Foundation of
Richmond, Virginia (AARF)*
www.aarf.org

Apache Junction, AZ, Animal Control
www.ajcity.net/index.asp?NID=266

Black Pearl Dogs
www.blackpearldogs.com

Compassion Without Borders
www.tdi-dog.org

Columbia-Greene Humane Society/SPCA
www.cghs.org

Evergreen Animal Protective League
www.eapl.com

Lone Star Lab Rescue
www.lonestarlabrescue.org

MidAmerica Border Collie Rescue
www.midamericabcrescue.com

Molly's Militia
www.mollysmilitia.org

Out of the Pits
www.outofthepits.org

Petfinder.com
www.petfinder.com

PetSmart Charities
www.petsmartcharities.org

Pets in Need
www.petsinneed.org

Pacific Northwest Border Collie Rescue
www.pnwbcrescue.org

Rhode Island SPCA
www.rispca.com

Second Chance Rescue
San Rafael, CA
www.animalshelter.org/shelters/Second_Chance_
Rescue_rId658_rS_pC.html

Tony La Russa's Animal Rescue Foundation
www.arf.net/index.php

Washington Animal Rescue League (WARL)
www.warl.org

OTHER ORGANIZATIONS MENTIONED IN THIS BOOK

Advanced K-9 Detectives
www.advancedk9detectives.com/about.html

Gilda's Club
www.gildasclub.org

Great Dog Camp K-9 for Kids
www.insidecamps.com/review/great-dog-camp-
k9-for-kids-3377.html

Kandu: Oh Yes, You Kandu!
www.kandu.us

Maureen's Music
www.maureensmusic.com

Nuts for Mutts Dog Show
www.nutsformutts.org

Orthopets
www.orthopets.com

Prison Pet Partnership
www.prisonpetpartnership.org/index.htm

Tellington Touch
www.ttouch.com

Washington Humane Society humane education program
www.washhumane.org/humaneeducation.asp

TERRIER FIELD TRIALS

The American Working Terrier Association
www.dirt-dog.com

Check the Internet for other activities such as Frisbee competition, herding, lure coursing, and skijoring/sledding. Don't forget walking, hiking, swimming, backpacking, and camping—all activities that are fun to share with a dog.

Recommended Reading

Adoption and Rescue

Bailey, Gwen. *Adopt the Perfect Dog: A Practical Guide to Choosing and Training an Adult Dog*. Reader's Digest, 2000.

Branigan, Cynthia A. *Adopting the Racing Greyhound*. Howell Book House, 1993.

Frost, Shelley and Katerina Lorenzatos Makris. *Your Adopted Dog: Everything You Need to Know About Rescuing and Caring for a Best Friend in Need*. Lyons Press, 2007.

Gonzalez, Philip and Lenore Fleischer. *The Dog Who Rescues Cats: The True Story of Ginny*. Harper Collins, 1995.

Gonzalez, Philip and Lenore Fleischer. *The Blessing of the Animals: True Stories of Ginny, the Dog Who Rescues Cats*. Perennial, 1997.

Hess, Elizabeth. *Lost and Found: Dogs, Cats, and Everyday Heroes at a Country Animal Shelter*. Harcourt Brace and Company, 1998.

Kerns, Nancy, ed. *The Whole Dog Journal Handbook of Dog and Puppy Care and Training*. Lyons Press, 2008.

Children's Books

Duncan, Susan. *Joey Moses*. Storytellers Ink, 1997.

Howey, Paul M. *Freckles: The Mystery of the Little White Dog in the Desert*. AZTexts Publishing Inc., 2003.

Pranghofer, Maureen. *Ally's Busy Day: The Story of a Service Dog*. Trafford Publishing, 2006.

Schieber, Barry J. *A Gift to Share: The Story of Moritz*. Silent Moon Books, 2005.

Human-Animal Bond

Becker, Dr. Marty. *The Healing Power of Pets: Harnessing the Amazing Ability of Pets to Make and Keep People Happy and Healthy*, Hyperion, 2003.

Katz, Jon. *Izzy and Lenore: Two Dogs, an Unexpected Journey, and Me*. Villard, 2008.

Lingenfelter, Mike and David Frei. *The Angel By My Side*. Hay House, 2002.

Rivera, Michelle A. *Canines in the Classroom: Raising Humane Children through Interactions with Animals*. Lantern Books, 2004.

Sakson, Sharon. *Paws & Effect: The Healing Power of Dogs*. Alyson Books, 2007.

Schoen, Allen M., D.V.M. *Kindred Spirits, How the Remarkable Bond Between Humans and Animals Can Change the Way We Live*. Broadway Books, 2001.

Magazines

Animal Fair magazine
  www.AnimalFair.com
The Bark, www.thebark.com
The Whole Dog Journal
  www.whole-dog-journal.com

Search and Rescue

American Rescue Dog Association. *Search and Rescue Dogs: Training Methods.* Howell Books, 1991.

American Rescue Dog Association. *Training the K-9 Hero.* Howell Books, 2002.

Training

Donaldson, Jean. *The Culture Clash.* James and Kenneth Publishing, 1997.

Dunbar, Ian. *Before You Get Your Puppy.* James and Kenneth Publishing, 2001.

———. *After You Get Your Puppy.* James and Kenneth Publishing, 2001.

Kilcommons, Brian and Sarah Wilson. *Childproofing Your Dog: A Complete Guide to Preparing Your Dog for the Children in Your Life.* Warner Books, 1994.

London, Karen B., PhD and Patricia McConnell, PhD. *Way to Go: How to House Train a Dog of Any Age.* Soft cover booklet available from Patricia McConnell, www.patriciamcconnell.com/product/way-to-go-how-to-house-train-a-dog-of-any-age/15

McConnell, Patricia B., PhD. *The Other End Of The Leash.* Ballantine Books, 2002.

McDevitt, Leslie, M.L.A., C.D.B.C., C.P.D.T. *Control Unleashed—Creating a Focused and Confident Dog.* Clean Run Productions, 2007.

Pelar, Colleen, C.P.D.T. *Living With Kids and Dogs . . . Without Losing Your Mind.* C & R Publishing, 2005.

Silvani, Pia, C.P.D.T. and Lynn Eckhardt. *Raising Puppies and Kids Together: A Guide for Parents.* T.F.H. Publications Inc., 2005.

Index